SEEING RED

Football's Most Violent Matches

SEEING RED

Football's Most Violent Matches

PHIL THOMPSON

First published 2006

STADIA is an imprint of
Tempus Publishing Limited
The Mill, Brimscombe Port,
Stroud, Gloucestershire, GL5 2QG
www.tempus-publishing.com

British Library Cataloguing in Publication Data.
A catalogue record for this book is available from the British Library.

ISBN 0 7524 3778 X

Typesetting and origination by Tempus Publishing Limited.
Printed in Great Britain.

INTRODUCTION

I was at the Everton *v.* Leeds match on 7 November 1964. The match was so violent that it became known as 'The Battle of Goodison Park'. From the kick-off both teams kicked lumps out of each other. Now I'd seen the great blond warrior Dave Hickson get involved in the odd fight leading the line for my local team Tranmere Rovers, but this was something else. It was as if both teams had declared war from the start. Don Revie's Leeds had just been promoted and they were clearly determined to show the big boys of the First Division that they were not in awe of them.

When I think back I have to admit I was frightened. I was just thirteen years old and I'd never witnessed grown men indulging in out-and-out violence. The spectators didn't know what was going to happen next as players seemed to be violently hacked down during every passage of play. The referee brought the game to a temporary halt and took the teams back to the dressing-rooms to cool down. It may have been sheer violence but, in a strange kind of way, it was also great theatre as well. In the same way that film footage of the infamous 1962 Chile *v.* Italy World Cup clash still makes compelling viewing.

Right from the beginning football has always produced its fair share of violent encounters. In 1886 Preston North End, who just two years later won the League and FA Cup double, were English football's first great team. Preston were outstanding, but they could certainly dish out the rough stuff if they were in the mood.

In one game against Blackburn Olympic, David Russell of Preston was seen to chase a Blackburn player halfway down the pitch and then land a severe kick to his back. This put the Blackburn player out of the match. A few weeks later Nick Ross of Preston despatched Blackburn's Jimmy Brown to hospital after a brutal hack at one of his legs. Brown was on the injured list for two months. Blackburn must have dreaded playing Preston during this era!

During the same year, Nick Ross's younger brother, Jimmy Ross, sparked a riot in an FA Cup tie between Queen's Park and Preston held at Hampden Park. During this period Queen's Park were the top team in Scotland. In order to participate in a higher standard of football than was possible in Scotland, Queen's Park elected to play games against English opposition. When Preston took on Queen's Park in their October 1886 match against Scotland's finest, the Lancashire club employed an, at times, quite brutal style of play. One writer remarked 'Preston North End, normally exponents of cultured and delicate football, forsook their normal style and battered their way to a 3–0 victory.'

With the game in the bag, Jimmy Ross of Preston hacked down the Queen's Park forward Harrower with a vicious tackle from behind. Harrower was carried from the pitch into the home team's dressing-room. The Queen's Park supporters had seen enough and when the final whistle blew, ran onto the field of play carrying sticks and umbrellas to use as weapons against the Preston team and Jimmy Ross in particular. The Preston team ran for their lives to the safety of the pavilion. With a mass of demonstrators waiting outside the Queen's Park pavilion for Preston to emerge, a back window was hastily opened and the Preston players escaped to safety.

Even in showpiece games such as FA Cup finals there would on occasions still be roughhouse tactics employed by teams desperate to win the trophy at all costs. A headline in *The Liverpool Daily Post and Mercury* after the 1907 FA Cup final read, 'Everton, the men of science, are defeated by Sheffield Wednesday, the men of muscle'. The report on the game went on to say:

At the Crystal Palace on Saturday, Everton, who may thus be classed as a highly civilised football combination because they are masters of the arts and refinements of the game, were overpowered by the men of muscle. In the majority of FA Cup ties man certainly slips back into a primitive state and thereby succeeds in overcoming the highest civilised state of football.

In the 1910 FA Cup final Newcastle and Barnsley fought out a 1–1 draw in a brutal encounter at the Crystal Palace, but if the final was violent, the replay was even worse. The replay took place at Goodison Park and the tackles were flying in right from the kick-off. Means, the Barnsley goalkeeper, was knocked out in the opening stages of the game after a violent challenge by Newcastle's Alex Higgins. In the second half, Dicky Downs of Barnsley, who had already sustained an injury to his leg in the first half, was kicked in the stomach and had to be carried from the pitch.

Newcastle won the replay 2-0, but long before the game reached its final stages, the crowd struck up a chant of 'Dirty Newcastle' to let the Newcastle team know what they thought of the dubious tactics they had employed in order to take the FA Cup back to Tyneside for the first time in their history.

In the 1913 final the FA Cup once again brought out the worst in two of England's top teams of the time, Aston Villa and Sunderland. Villa won the trophy 1-0 in a game littered with fierce tackling and foul play. *The Times*' football correspondent said of the game:

What was chiefly to be regretted was the ill-feeling which expressed itself in countless acts unworthy of sportsmen. One of the Sunderland half-backs was the worst offender. It was not his fault that Hampton of Villa did not leave the ground on a stretcher, but there was little to choose between the two sides in this respect. Aston Villa did not live up to their historic reputation for playing a clean sportsmanlike game. It is a grave pity that the most popular match of the year should opt to supply the crowd with so many object lessons in the tactics of foul play and ill-conditioned manners.

This brief summary of some of the violent encounters that took place in the early years of professional football gives one an insight into the fact that right from its early history, football fans would often witness brutal matches taking place. This book does not set out to glorify or trivialise violence on the field of play. Many unfortunate players have, after all, had their careers blighted or, in some instances, finished altogether by football thuggery, but the matches in this book did happen. There does seem to be a reluctance to discuss the more unsavoury aspects of the game's history by football historians past and present. Violence on and off the field of play has always taken place. Unpalatable though it may seem, it is a part of football history. We cannot pretend that it never occurred. After all, when you think of it, Lee Bowyer's bust-up with his teammate Kieron Dyer during the notorious 2005 encounter between Newcastle and Aston Villa will probably still be a topic of conversation with football followers long after everything else that happened at St James' Park during the 2004/05 football season is long forgotten.

Phil Thompson, 2006

THE MATCHES

FIASCO AT MIDDLESBROUGH

Middlesbrough 4-1 Oldham Athletic
Easter Monday, 1915
(match abandoned)

The Oldham Evening Chronicle described the game as 'A Fiasco at Ayresome Park'. Oldham were in the running for the First Division title, but on a heavy, rain-sodden pitch found themselves two goals down after only fifteen minutes. Tempers began to fray when an Oldham appeal for a penalty was turned down. With the Oldham players surrounding the referee to protest against his decision, Middlesbrough calmly took the ball upfield unopposed and slotted in number three. After that all hell broke loose with Oldham deciding to inflict their own retribution on their north-eastern opponents. One startled reporter described the remainder of the game thus:

> The whole proceedings were chilling to the nerves of an onlooker. So quickly did one ugly incident follow another that it was difficult to chronicle them all. Players ran riot, losing their heads and hurling themselves into each other. I had a continual fear that the climax would be the maiming of a player by the breaking of a limb or some other mishap.

The second half followed the same violent pattern of play and matters came to a head when the referee ordered Oldham full-back Billy Cook off for a foul on Carr. Cook refused to leave the field of play and the referee was left with no other option than to abandon the game. Interviewed after the game, the referee, Mr Smith, said, 'I gave Cook one minute to get off the field. I told him if he didn't, I would have to abandon the match. He still refused to go and I had no option but to end the game.' Incensed Middlesbrough supporters, totalling over 1,000, waited to confront the Oldham players after the game. Much to the Lancashire team's relief, they were smuggled out of the ground by another exit and whisked to safety. After an inquiry, the Football League fined Oldham £350 and banned Billy Cook for one year. The result was allowed to stand.

RUMPUS AT THE LANE

Tottenham Hotspur 1-2 Arsenal
23 September 1922

The relationship between north London rivals Arsenal and Spurs has been frosty right from the start. There were even claims in 1928 that Arsenal actually threw games in order to try and get Spurs relegated. Until the legendary Herbert Chapman arrived at Arsenal in 1925 and turned them into one of the nation's top clubs, Spurs were definitely the governors of north London.

In an era when brutal tackling, either from the front or behind, was regarded as the norm, this north London derby must have been a particularly bruising encounter. Two players were sent off, a rare occurrence indeed during this period, with twenty players receiving their marching orders in the whole of the English League season being the average. Several players also sustained injuries that rendered them as virtual passengers for the rest of the game. Repercussions after the match led to an FA Commission of Inquiry, suspensions and censures.

Spurs' problems began as early as the tenth minute when Walden broke down with a leg injury. He left the pitch and did not return. Bliss of the home team then also sustained a leg injury and he was reduced to hobbling about on the wing for the rest of the game. Spurs were then reduced to eight fit men when Hutchins clattered into Lindsay. Lindsay returned to the field however and appeared to be none the worse for the incident.

The White Hart Lane crowd, who had been in a state of high excitement throughout the game, became positively hostile to the Arsenal team after Boreham put the away team into the lead. Ten minutes from the finish Boreham scored Arsenal's second. Spurs hit back on the stroke of full-time when Lindsay ran through to beat the static Arsenal defence and score. Several of the Arsenal team had actually made no attempt to stop Lindsay scoring, thinking that the referee had blown for offside. When the referee waved away their protests and gave the goal, the Arsenal players blew their tops. Their protests were described by one reporter as 'deplorable.' After the game the hostilities carried on in the streets surrounding the ground and there were reports of skirmishes between rival supporters.

THE BATTLE OF HIGHBURY

England 3–2 Italy
14 November 1934

England captain Eddie Hapgood described this encounter as 'the dirtiest game I ever played in'. Italy's Fascist leader Benito Mussolini was desperate for a victory over England, who had never been defeated on home soil by foreign opposition. Huge financial incentives were up for grabs to the Italians, who were the reigning world champions after winning the second World Cup in Italy during the summer tournament. The propaganda value of a win over England had been made patently clear to the Italian team before the game by the Fascist government and they were determined to win at all costs.

After only two minutes, Italy defender Monti broke his foot after clashing with Arsenal's Ted Drake. This set the tone for the rest of the match. The Italians were unhappy with Drake's challenge on Monti and sought retribution for the remaining eighty-eight minutes. Arsenal hardman Wilf Copping, who was the most feared player in British football at the time, decided to play the Italians at their own game. George Male recalled, 'The Italians were petrified of Wilf. He was practically playing them on his own at the finish.' The Italians fought back well in the second half but England held on to take the game 3-2.

Why the Swedish referee refrained from dismissing from the field of play the perpetrators of such violent conduct remains one of football's great mysteries. The Highbury dressing-rooms resembled a hospital casualty ward after the match as both teams became embroiled in probably the most violent encounter ever to take place on English soil. Eddie Hapgood, when asked by England why he did not refrain from getting involved in the violence retorted, 'It was difficult to play like a gentleman when somebody closely resembling an enthusiastic member of the Mafia is wiping his studs down your leg.'

Stanley Matthews reflected later:

> I was only nineteen and it was one of the roughest games of my life. Hapgood had his nose broken and was taken off. It was fortunate that in Brook and Copping we had a couple of tough nuts who were able to respond with the honest shoulder charge.

Arsenal secretary Bob Wall said:

> Just before half-time Wilf Copping tackled one of the Italian inside forwards so hard that both the Arsenal doctor and the Italian medical officer were hurriedly summoned to examine the poor fellow. At half-time Wilf was walking along the corridor beneath the stand when he met our doctor. 'How's that Eytie?' enquired Wilf. 'Oh! He won't come back,' replied the doctor. 'Bloody good job. He'd soon be back in the dressing-room,' came the instant response.

THE DAY IT RAINED BOTTLES

Rangers 3–0 Celtic
6 September 1941

The *Sunday Post* described this bruising 1941 Old Firm encounter as 'a riot of a game'. Bottles rained down on to the pitch as players kicked lumps out of each other on it. Police fought with the rioting sections of the 60,000 crowd after a penalty was awarded to Celtic. Baton-drawn police were met with a hail of flying glass as they tried to break up the feuding fans.

Up until the penalty decision, the action had been fast and furious and, uniquely for a Rangers–Celtic game, in the main without violent incident. After the penalty, which Celtic missed, all hell broke loose. Delaney and Crum of Celtic were both stretchered off as the tackling grew fiercer by the minute. The fighting on the terraces continued to escalate and mounted police were brought into the action in an attempt to quell the violence. Many were arrested and a uniformed soldier was amongst the casualties who were stretchered out of the ground for treatment.

After the interval the game degenerated into one foul after another as the tackles became increasingly dangerous. This was the first Old Firm meeting of the season and as one writer put it, 'The people of Glasgow and the Clydeside shipyards are suffering violence from the sky inflicted by the German Luftwaffe, while fans at the Old Firm game insisted on bottle-throwing aerial intimidation of their own.'

Rangers won the game 3–0 in one of the most violent Glasgow derbies so far, but there would be plenty more to come.

ANOTHER OLD FIRM RIOT

Celtic 0–2 Rangers
Victory Cup semi-final
5 June 1946

Even by Old Firm standards this has to go down as one of the most sensational of all time. In a violent encounter, two Celtic players were sent off, a spectator armed with a bottle attacked the referee, police fought with spectators on the pitch and fights were breaking out at regular intervals on the terraces. Trouble flared after the referee awarded Rangers a penalty kick.

The referee, local man Mr M. Dale, was then surrounded by protesting Celtic players. George Young of Rangers stepped up to take the spot-kick but the Celtic players refused to step aside to allow him to take it. Paterson of Celtic was then ordered off the pitch. This had no effect on his colleagues, who still would not allow the kick to be taken. Celtic full-back Malton was then also sent off. It appeared at one stage that the Celtic team were about to walk off the field, but after much argument, the kick was allowed to be taken. Young's penalty put Rangers 2–0 in the lead, a lead they would keep until the end of the game.

With the game just about to restart, a spectator ran on to the pitch brandishing a bottle and aimed several blows at the referee. The match official managed to dodge his attacker, but other spectators had now invaded the pitch and were imploring the Celtic players to walk off. These were then tackled by a contingent of policemen. As all this was happening, fights were breaking out on the terraces and the police had their work cut out to control the situation.

Eventually, the game did reach its conclusion, Celtic finishing with only eight men after Gallagher had been carried off with a leg injury. Players from both Celtic and Rangers had been sent off in previous games but this was the first time two had been dismissed in one game. An enquiry resulted in Paterson and Mallon receiving three-month suspensions from the game. Another Celtic player, Matt

Lynch, received a four-game ban after being booked at the end of the game. Rangers' Jimmy Duncanson even sent a testimony to the Scottish Football Association claiming that Matt Lynch was innocent of any misdemeanour, but this was ignored. Celtic, during this period, claimed that the Scottish FA had it in for them. The general consensus at the time was that Celtic's claims of prejudice against them by the Scottish football authorities were correct. Apparently, the flying of the Irish tricolour by Celtic supporters did not go down well with some members of the SFA, with Eire's neutral stance during the Second World War still fresh in the memory.

THE BATTLE OF BERNE

Hungary 4-2 Brazil
World Cup quarter-final
27 July 1954

English referee Arthur Ellis described this match between the two giants of world football as 'the toughest of my life'. A feast of great football was anticipated. Hungary, after all, were clear favourites for the World Cup and widely regarded as the best team in the world. The match, however, lived long in the memory as one of the most brutal World Cup games of all time. The brilliant Hungarians were two goals up within the first seven minutes. Brazil, clearly shaken, decided the best way to knock the Hungarians out of their stride would be through violence.

It was in the second half that the game really exploded. One vicious tackle followed another and when Bozsik, Hungary's half-back who was also a member of the Hungarian Parliament, and Brazilian man-mountain Nilton Santos decided to exchange punches, referee Ellis sent them both off. After that it was a free-for-all, with football only a secondary consideration. The match became a running fight and at one stage even the legendary Ferenc Puskas, who was not playing due to injury, left his seat in the stand to join in the fight. A few minutes from time, with Hungary now leading 4-2, Humberto of Brazil also received his marching orders. Hungary's place in the semi-final of the World Cup was now guaranteed, but in many ways it was a hollow victory.

At the final whistle, the fighting continued with spectators now becoming involved. Pinheiro of Brazil collapsed, apparently after being hit with an iron bar. Eager for revenge, the Brazilian team invaded the Hungarian dressing-room, breaking down the door in the process, and attacked the Hungarians. Puskas was seen fighting desperately with one of the Brazilians. Hungary's Minister of Sport Gustav Sebes, who was also Hungary's team manager, was among the many who received head wounds. The fighting only came to an end when Swiss police rushed to the scene and managed to separate the warring factions.

Don Ateyo, an English observer at the game, described what happened:

> The Brazilians stormed the Hungarian dressing-room where there ensued the extraordinary spectacle of two dozen international players battering each other with boots and liniment bottles amid jock straps and dirty sweaters. The worst casualty was a Hungarian who had his cheek laid open.

Another eyewitness account alleged that Puskas smashed Pinheiro in the face with a bottle. In the general melee that took place, what actually did and didn't take place became somewhat blurred. Pinheiro, however, was seen leaving the ground with his head swathed in bandages.

BLOODBATH AT GRESTY ROAD

Crewe Alexandra 2-1 Bradford Park Avenue
8 January 1955

A Third Division encounter at Crewe's Gresty Road ground is not the occasion one would expect for one of the most sensational – in terms of violence and sendings-off – games of the 1950s. By all accounts the first half was quite an uneventful affair, with Crewe going in at the interval with a two-goal lead. God knows what was put into the tea during the break, but within minutes of the restart the game took a violent turn for the worse.

Samuels of Crewe and Bradford's Horton became embroiled in a no-holds-barred fist fight before they both fell to the rain-sodden turf, still aiming blows at each other. Players from both teams rushed to separate the mud-covered pair and referee S. Bostock took their names and sent both of them off.

After that, the game developed into a series of scything tackles and was described in the local Crewe paper as more like a scrapping match than a football match. It was every man for himself as bone-crunching tackles caused a long series of stoppages. Although not of the same quality as the Samuels–Horton bout earlier in the half, another fist fight inevitably did flare up with Wright of Bradford and Crewe's McGuigan laying into each other eight minutes from the final whistle. The referee sent the two of them off and then called all the players together to give them a stern lecture.

By this time the crowd, following the lead of the players on the pitch, were also in a violent frame of mind and the game ended to a crescendo of boos, cat-calls and whistles. For the first time in the history of the Football League four players had been sent off in a single game. Crewe took the points with a 2-1 victory.

Note: This record was beaten in 1997 when, on 22 February, five players were sent off in a match between Chesterfield and Plymouth Argyle match. On 20 December 1997 the record was equalled during a Wigan *v.* Bristol Rovers game. Hereford created a League record of their own on 11 November 1992 when they had four players from the same team sent off in a game.

DUEL IN THE SUN

Spain 1-1 England
18 May 1955

A 125,000 crowd at the Chamartin Stadium in Madrid witnessed this match. The game was eagerly anticipated in Spain and England were looking to avenge their first defeat on the Continent, which had occurred in the same city some twenty-six years previously. But the game turned out to be a bruising encounter. The football correspondent of *The Times* wrote, 'This game was anticipated as the greatest sporting event in Spain for a quarter of a century, but it proved to be the stormiest, shabbiest match England have ever contested. There was too much that was positively ugly.'

Most of the violence occurred after England took the lead against the run of play in the thirty-ninth minute. Roy Bentley blasted in the opening goal from the edge of the penalty area and this sent the fiercely partisan crowd into a stunned silence. Just before half-time, Nat Lofthouse was sent through and just as he was about to take aim, Garay rugby-tackled him two yards short of the penalty area. Lofthouse later remarked, 'I've played in some hard games, but there were times during the Spain game when I wondered if they'd got our match mixed up with the fight scheduled later in the week in the nearby bullring.'

In the second half, Spain fought like tigers to get back on level terms and both teams resorted to dubious methods as they fought for supremacy. The gulf in what were viewed as acceptable ball-winning tactics between the British and the Continentals was never more evident than during this game. To the British, shoulder charging and hard tackling were part and parcel of football. To the Continentals, obstruction and nudging to win possession was equally acceptable. Stanley Matthews, in particular, was given a torrid time in the second half as he was singled out for some violent treatment. At one stage, even the normally placid Matthews lost his cool as he was kicked to the ground for the ump-teenth time. As the battered wing wizard lay on the ground receiving treatment, he turned to England's goal hero Roy Bentley and said, 'I've had enough of this full-back, I could spit at him.' 'Stanley,' replied Roy, 'spit at him? Never mind spitting at him, bloody well kick him back.' Eventually Spain's frenetic pursuit for an equaliser paid off and the game, one of the most violent in England's history, ended all square.

BOXING DAY FISTICUFFS

Dartford 2–0 Gravesend & Northfleet
Southern League
Boxing Day 1959
(match abandoned)

Not necessarily one of the most violent encounters of the century, according to those who witnessed this Boxing Day local derby, but most certainly one of the most infamous. Mr A.J. Sturgeon, who was the match referee, abandoned the game ten minutes from the end after sending off the whole twenty-two players. The spectators at Dartford's rain-lashed Watling Street ground could not believe what they were witnessing.

It had been a typical hard-fought local derby with the tackles flying in thick and fast. With eighty minutes on the clock, a Dartford player went down injured and the referee stopped the play to allow him to receive treatment. It was while the trainer was on the field of play that Mr Sturgeon blew two long blasts on his whistle and then motioned to the startled players that the game was over. It was the first time in football history that the whole twenty-two players had been dismissed from the field of play. After the game, referee Sturgeon was adamant that he had made the correct decision. He told reporters, 'A Dartford player was punched in the stomach and other players were fighting among themselves. I decided to take strong action and I am standing by my decision. I don't regret it for one moment.' After the game, an angry crowd outside the ground began to chant, 'we want our money back', but it was not forthcoming.

Although the game was the first time all twenty-two players had been sent off, a wartime encounter between Crystal Palace and Millwall on 28 September 1940 also saw both teams taken from the field of play. The referee, however, brought the two teams back out after a 'cooling down' period and the game was resumed.

THE BATTLE OF SANTIAGO

Chile 2-0 Italy
World Cup
4 June 1962

Chile, the host nation for the 1962 World Cup Finals, won this game 2-0, but in many ways football was of secondary importance in this, one of the most infamous matches of all time. The violent tone was set before the game had even begun when newspaper articles written by Italian journalists claimed that Chile as a country was a dump.

From the kick-off, both teams began to kick lumps out of each other. Italy's Ferrini and Chile's Sanchez exchanged kicks. A minute later, Ferrini and Chile's Lander became embroiled in another violent clash. English referee Ken Aston sent off Ferrini, who at first refused to leave the field. Nearly ten minutes had gone by before a weeping Ferrini was led away by Italian officials and armed police.

Referee Aston and his officials found it virtually an impossible task to control the violence that was taking place and none of the officials saw Leonel Sanchez of Chile pull himself to his feet, after being brought down in a heavy challenge, and knock the offending Italian out cold with a left hook. Sanchez, the son of a professional boxer, had broken the Italian's nose. Aston and his officials failed to act, which led to accusations after the game that much of the trouble could have been avoided with stronger refereeing. The incensed Italians were determined to make Sanchez pay and decided to take matters into their own hands. With half-time approaching, David of Italy hit Sanchez with a head-high tackle. David was immediately ordered off. Once again it took officials and police to persuade the player to leave.

In the second half, Maschio of Italy also sustained a broken nose after a clash with Rojas. In the final minute of the game, Toro of Chile looked like he would become the third player to be sent off after becoming involved in a scuffle. Referee Aston gestured to send him off and once again police and officials ran on to the pitch, but then Aston decided against it and picked up the ball, whistled to signify the end of the game and disappeared to the dressing-rooms. In the

Referee Ken Aston sends off Italy's Mario David after the Italian had poleaxed Chile's Leonel Sanchez with a high tackle. The 1962 World Cup encounter between the two countries was one of the most sensational games of all time.

aftermath of the game, the Italians had to be guarded by armed air force personnel and in bars and shops in the city notices sprang up stating, 'No Italians admitted'. One Chilean dignitary, Judge Jorga Pica, said after the game, 'Frankly, I think the Italians were doped for they seemed out of control. They only wanted to hurt their opponents and not play football. Their whole attitude was abnormal and it proves to me the need for laboratory tests for all players after a match.'

Interviewed recently, Leonel Sanchez, the hard man of Chilean football, said he does have some regrets about his actions. He said:

> Their defender David came in and kicked me, and I fell to the ground. He kept on kicking me to try and get the ball that was trapped between my feet. So I stood up and clocked him. I think you regret something like that the moment you do it. I could have got sent off and left my team a man short. I ended up going to Milan to play in the same team as David, the player whose nose I had broken. We became great friends.

THE BATTLE OF BELGRADE

OFK Belgrade 1-2 Tottenham Hotspur
European Cup-Winners' Cup semi-final
24 April 1963

In the early 1960s, Spurs were undoubtedly the greatest team in the land. Their domination of the English game may have only lasted a couple of seasons, but Bill Nicholson's fabulous 'Double' winning team of 1961 gave their fans one final moment of glory before disbanding. In 1963 Tottenham became the first British club to win a major European trophy. Their victory over Atletico Madrid in the 1963 European Cup-Winners' Cup final in Rotterdam brought down the curtain on the Spurs career of their inspirational captain Danny Blanchflower.

In the final itself, Jimmy Greaves scored two goals in Spurs 5-1 victory over the Spaniards, but in the semi-finals it was an altogether different story for the London club's ace goalscorer. During the away leg of the semi against OFK Belgrade, Greaves became the first Spurs player to be dismissed since Cecil Poynton was sent off in 1928.

The game itself was a quite brutal affair with OFK determined to use brute force in an attempt to nullify the superior (in terms of footballing ability) Spurs team. The game was played in front of a passionate 50,000 crowd at the Army Stadium in Belgrade. Spurs actually used the ploy of a double centre-half pairing of Norman and Marchi to ward off the threat of the expected early onslaught by OFK. When it came to the rough stuff, Norman and Marchi, along with Spurs' resident enforcers of Dave Mackay in midfield and Bobby Smith up front, were certainly a match for anything physical that the Slavs could throw at them.

The first real flare-up came after twenty-five minutes when a melee just outside the OFK penalty threatened to develop into a full-scale brawl. The Hungarian referee struggled to maintain order, but when the dust settled Spurs took the lead from the resulting free-kick. Bobby Smith passed to John White, who hit a piledriver from the edge of the penalty area to give Spurs the lead.

Amid the storm of whistles and catcalls emanating from the OFK fans that packed the terraces, which greeted the Spurs goal, there was a strange occurrence. During this era, unlike in the modern-day game, very few football followers travelled abroad to support their club, but on this bitterly cold night in Belgrade the strains of 'The Spurs Go Marching On' could clearly be heard coming from the terraces. It turned out that the unexpected group of Spurs fans were a party of actors and backroom staff who were making a film, *The Long Ships*, at a nearby location. All were dressed as Vikings and they had even borrowed the directors' megaphones in their efforts to cheer on the London club.

In the second half OFK, who had equalised just before the half-time interval, pushed forward desperately looking for a lead to take to White Hart Lane for the return leg. Their tackling grew more fierce and Spurs' danger man Jimmy Greaves was on the receiving end of most of it. With the second period just ten minutes old, Greaves lashed out after one of the OFK players threw a punch at him. To this day Greaves insists that the referee got the wrong man. He said, 'Going for a ball, Bobby Smith caught their centre-half in the stomach with his elbow. It really took the wind out of the bloke. This fella then jumps up and comes at me like a bull. He threw a punch and missed. I immediately threw one back and missed.'

The referee decided that Greaves was the guilty party and sent him off. As he walked to the touchline he was greeted by an array of bottles and anything else that the OFK fans could lay their hands on. Greaves was quickly ushered to the dressing-room out of harm's way. The strange thing is the fact that the Spurs trainer at the time was Cecil Poynton, the last Spurs player to be sent off, back in 1928. It was Poynton who guided Greaves to the sanctuary of the dressing-room in Belgrade.

After Jimmy Greaves' dismissal Spurs went on to produce one of their greatest European displays and won the game through a Terry Dyson goal. By the end the Belgrade fans had even turned on their own team and began to jeer every pass by OFK.

The press, though quick to praise Spurs for their gallant display, were unanimous in their condemnation of OFK and the poor refereeing of the game. The football correspondent for the *Daily Telegraph* remarked, 'Once more we were confronted by the two philosophies of how football should be played and the wide and different interpretations set upon the laws by foreign referees! One has seen it before and one will see it again, unfortunately.'

After Spurs won the return leg 3-1 to progress to the final in another physical encounter, *The Times* said of the match, 'There remained some ruthless and cruel tackling that we had first seen in Belgrade. Victory, at times, would seem to cost too much a price in dignity. It is human, I suppose, and understandable, but at moments animal instincts seem to creep in.'

HAMPDEN PARK BRUTALITY

Scotland 4-1 Austria
8 May 1963
(match abandoned)

Amid some of the most astonishing scenes ever witnessed in a football match in Britain, English referee Jim Finney abandoned the game fifteen minutes from the end of this game at Hampden Park. The trouble began midway through the first half when Nemec, Austria's giant fifteen-stone centre-forward objected to Scotland's second goal. Nemec continued to harangue referee Finney as the kick-off for the game's restart was about to be taken. It was alleged that he spat in the direction of Finney and was threatening to take his protest to a more physical level. Fearing for his safety Finney ordered Nemec off the pitch and was immediately surrounded by Nemec's Austrian teammates. At one stage, players and officials from both countries became involved in a heated altercation and order was only restored when Nemec agreed to return to the dressing-room.

After that, the Austrian tackling became more aggressive but, in Mackay, Ure and Denis Law, Scotland also had players who could mix it when needed. With two goals apiece from Wilson and Law, Scotland, despite Austria's strong-arm tactics, appeared to be heading for a comfortable victory. The tackling from both teams had been vicious throughout with many verbal threats being exchanged. With the game entering its closing stages, the referee attempted to order off Austria's inside forward Hof for a deliberate kick on one of the Scotland players. Hof refused to go and once again there followed much heated discussion between the referee, officials and police before Hof left the pitch. At one stage, a policeman had to protect referee Finney when an Austrian reserve rushed at the bewildered official from the bench.

Just minutes later, Denis Law decided to indulge himself in the open brutality that was going on all around him when he hit Linhart with a ferocious tackle. It was while Linhart was being carried off the pitch that the referee decided he had seen enough. He walked to the touchline, told the officials of both Scotland and Austria that he was abandoning the game. It was left up to the police to tell the two teams that the game was over and that they should leave the pitch. Speaking after the match, Mr Finney told reporters, 'I sent off Nemec for spitting and Hof for a diabolical waistline foul. I stopped the game because there was no telling how it was going to end. It was getting completely out of control. Somebody might have been seriously injured.'

RIOT IN LIMA

Peru 0–1 Argentina
Olympic Games qualifier
25 May 1964

The greatest disaster in football history occurred at the National Stadium in Lima, Peru on the 25 May 1964. The death toll was 318 with a further 500 injured. The two teams were playing for a place at the Olympic Games that were to be held in Tokyo later that year, so the stakes were high. Over 45,000 packed the stadium to witness the contest between the two South American countries.

Argentina were expected to triumph and, despite the tense atmosphere and hostile home crowd, who jeered every decision that went against Peru, the away team looked like they would hold out for a narrow victory. A draw would have put Peru through, but Argentina were leading 1-0 with just two minutes to play. Then Peru broke away and scored what looked to be an equaliser.

The referee, to the amazement of the crowd, disallowed the goal for a foul by one of the Peru team in the build-up. This was the signal for a couple of the spectators to rush onto the field of play to attack the referee. The police came to the official's assistance, but more angry spectators began to invade the pitch.

Fearing for the safety of the two teams, as well as himself and the two other officials, the referee, Angel Pazos, ordered the game to be suspended. When the decision was announced through the loudspeakers the spectators became hysterical and began to climb over the barriers surrounding the pitch to attack the officials and the players. The referee and players ran for cover to the tunnels leading to the dressing-rooms. A small contingent of police held the rioting spectators at bay long enough for the officials and teams to be quickly herded on to a waiting bus that drove them away from the stadium still in their football strips.

Police on horseback then attempted to clear the rioters from the pitch by directing them to the exits. Some of the police then began firing shots into the air and teargas grenades exploded near the spectators fleeing the stadium. This caused a mass panic, which was intensified when many of the spectators found that the exits from the stadium were locked. Many were trampled as mobs of people surged forward. The police then set their dogs on the terrified spectators, which made the situation even more chaotic. At least four fans were shot dead by the police, with the majority of the other deaths being caused by asphyxiation.

At this stage angry mobs began to smash up the stadium and once out into the streets surrounding the arena they carried on with their riotous behaviour. Cars were overturned or set on fire and shops and buildings were looted. As mounted police fought to restore order, more buildings were set on fire in a scene of complete mayhem. Most of those that died were trampled to death near the stadium exits. As people lay dying on the ground, gangs of youths stole watches, jewellery and wallets from their persons.

In the centre of Lima the rioting spread, with buses, cars, office blocks and shops looted and set on fire. Another mob marched to the National Palace to seek an audience with the President of Peru. They wanted him to intervene and have the game declared as a draw to allow Peru to get through to the Olympic Games. The Government immediately declared a state of emergency and martial law was in force for thirty days after the riot took place.

THE BATTLE OF GOODISON PARK

Everton 0–1 Leeds United
7 November 1964

Don Revie's newly promoted Leeds United were determined not to be overawed by their more illustrious First Division opponents and this ethos was never more evident than during this bruising encounter. The tone was set after only five minutes when Johnny Giles and Sandy Brown clashed. Giles recalled, 'We collided in challenging for the ball. Brown wriggled free, leapt to his feet and aimed a punch at my head.' Brown was sent off and after that it was all downhill. The tackling got fiercer by the minute. Tough little Everton winger Johnny Morrissey, who even Liverpool's legendary hard man Tommy Smith was wary of, recalled the game:

> Paul Reaney was marking me. Early in the game, I got an elbow in the face from him. He said next time he was going to do this and that to me. I said, 'Fair enough.' Leeds actually started all the gamesmanship in the First Division after their promotion. They would talk to the referee throughout the game and were diving everywhere.

Matters came to a head after thirty-seven minutes when Leeds full-back Willie Bell thundered into Everton's Derek Temple with a fierce two-footed tackle. Temple was carried off on a stretcher. Bell was also carried to the sidelines by his teammates. The Goodison Park crowd were by this stage going berserk and referee Ken Stokes decided to bring the proceedings to a temporary halt by taking both teams off the field of play to cool down.

After a ten-minute break, the teams returned to the field, but throughout the remainder of the game, the threat of further violence was never far away. The fact that Norman Hunter was the only player to be booked in the second half was nothing short of amazing and an example of how lenient referees were in the 1960s. Leeds' 1-0 victory was probably their most impressive result since their return to the First Division. Leeds' Jack Charlton was in no doubt after the game that it was the hostile Everton supporters who had whipped up the players into such a frenzy. He said, 'Both teams were equally to blame for on-field incidents but the Goodison Park crowd is the worst I have ever played before. There always seems to be a threatening attitude, a vicious undertone to their remarks.' Johnny Giles was of the same opinion. He remarked, 'Referee Stokes was pelted with rubbish by the Everton supporters after he halted play. It was the most frightening moment I have ever experienced on a football pitch. I thought all 55,000 spectators were going to invade the pitch at one stage.' Billy Bremner also once said it was one of the roughest games he had ever played in: 'The tackles were going in as if it was a matter of life and death. There were professional footballers out there who had completely forgotten what they were there for. The ball was getting in the way of revenge missions.'

Jack Charlton also told the following story:

Our goalkeeper, Gary Sprake, was picking up so many coins from the pitch – coins thrown from the crowd – that at full-time when we asked him how much he had got, he turned round and said, 'I don't really know – I could have got more, but I only picked up the silver.

Billy Bremner spoke of Leeds United's reputation at this time, saying, 'We had to get used to hearing people say we had kicked our way out of the Second Division. Because we went in for the ball hard we became tagged "Dirty Leeds".'

THE X-RATED SEMI-FINAL

Manchester United 0-0 Leeds United
FA Cup semi-final
27 March 1965
(Leeds won the replay 1-0)

'This wasn't a match. It was a brawl that needed a lion-tamer, not a referee, to control it' was just one of the indignant comments to feature in the match reports of this violent Manchester United–Leeds cup-tie. 'It was a disgrace and right now I'm going to name the guilty men,' proclaimed another paper. 'They are Bremner, Collins, Hunter, Storrie and Jack Charlton of Leeds, and Law, Stiles, Crerand, Connelly and Bobby Charlton of Manchester United.' Bobby Charlton! It must have been rough! Taking place on a muddy Hillsborough pitch that looked like something from The Somme, this encounter turned out to be one of the most ugly in FA Cup history.

It was Denis Law who started the ball rolling when the fiery Scot appeared to headbutt Jack Charlton. Charlton squared up to Law and a free-for-all soon developed as players rushed to join in the fray. Bremner, Collins, Hunter, Crerand and Stiles all became involved in a mass brawl, but amazingly in those lenient days of the 1960s no names were taken. Earlier in the game Law had found himself in the referee's notebook after a violent tackle on Willie Bell. Nobby Stiles also went into the book for bringing Leeds' winger Johanneson down. The remainder of the game was a series of kicks, trips and punches as the game reached an ugly climax. Denis Law, who had already served a one-month suspension that season for misconduct on the pitch, was considered lucky not to have gone for an early bath as both teams battled for a place in the FA Cup final.

Asked about the game recently, Jack Charlton said, 'That was one match that I want to forget. In fact, I can't remember anything good about it.' Denis Law, in fact, ended the game with his shirt ripped from collar to chest after a wrestling match with Jack Charlton. Every ball was fought for as if each player's life depended on not allowing the opposition an inch. The game ended in a 0-0 draw, but the repercussions in the media went on for weeks. Leeds boss Don Revie and his Manchester United counterpart Matt Busby were blamed for not controlling their teams. The referee, Dick Windle, also came in for stern criticism for being too lenient with the Leeds and Manchester United players

The replay, four days later, was another confrontational affair, with Dick Windle once again in charge. The levels of violence in the game, played at Nottingham, did not however reach the same scale as the first match. A headed goal by the outstanding Billy Bremner, two minutes from time, sent Leeds to Wembley. As the players left the pitch at the end of the game there was more drama as the referee was pushed to the ground and remained there for some time in a dazed condition. The guilty fan was apprehended by the police, but Manchester United and Leeds had once again hit the headlines for all the wrong reasons. Johnny Giles later said:

> Nobby Stiles [Giles' brother-in-law] and I have always been extremely close, which has prompted a number of people to ask what goes through my mind when I have to tackle him, or vice versa. We did clash at Hillsborough. In the second half we went into a strong tackle for a 50/50 ball. Nobby slumped to the ground clutching his right leg. As he lay there, motionless, I was convinced that he had sustained a serious injury. I felt sick, and started to cry [Stiles had been out for months after a cartilage operation]. I heard United's Pat Crerand shout: 'Don't worry John, he's OK.' No words can describe my feelings of relief.

THE BATTLE OF STAMFORD BRIDGE

Chelsea 4–1 Roma
Inter-Cities Fairs Cup
22 September 1965

Tommy Docherty's outstanding young Chelsea side of the 1960s found themselves in Europe for the first time at the start of the 1965/66 season. Chelsea's early adventures were to prove somewhat traumatic. They were drawn against Italian team Roma in their first game and the two ties were to prove violent encounters.

Chelsea's tough full-back Eddie McCreadie had been involved in a physical battle with Roma's Leonardi from the kick-off. McCreadie, who had had his shin split open after an over-the-top tackle from

Chelsea's Ron 'Chopper' Harris with his manager Tommy Docherty. Harris was Docherty's enforcer in the Chelsea team. Their matches against Roma in 1965 rank among the most violent games in the club's history.

Leonardi, was also then grabbed by the Roma forward in a vice-like grip that the Boston Strangler would have been proud of. Finally, McCreadie snapped and hit Leonardi with a right hook that left the Italian out cold.

The Scot was sent off and left the field in tears, but the violence did not end there. Terry Venables, who scored a sensational hat-trick on the night, found himself having to be taken off the field for treatment after an x-rated tackle from Barison, for which the Roma player had his name taken. Chelsea had to play out the rest of the first half with only nine men.

Venables returned after the break and Chelsea increased their lead to take a three-goal advantage to Italy for the return leg. Tommy Docherty described the game as the most disgraceful he had ever seen and although his team had a three-goal cushion he was not looking forward to the return game in Rome with any relish. Ron Harris later said:

> They call me 'Chopper Harris', but believe me, when I saw some of the tactics used by players on the Continent I reckon I am almost a soccer angel. They're the choppers of football, not the British players. There is a world of difference in our attitude to the game. That is why I believe there will always be trouble when we meet.

THE BATTLE OF ROME

Roma 0–0 Chelsea
Inter–Cities Fairs Cup
6 October 1965

With a hate campaign conducted by the Italian press against the London club in full flow, it was with a great degree of trepidation that Chelsea touched down at Rome Airport to face the wounded, and eager for revenge, Roma side. Eddie McCreadie, who had decked Roma favourite Leonardi and got sent off in the Stamford Bridge first-leg tie, was the main object of the Italians' venom.

The team bus which took the Chelsea side to Roma's Flaminio Stadium was jeered and spat at as it made its way to the ground. When the Chelsea party walked on to the pitch before the game they were subjected to a torrent of abuse as well as having bottles, rotten fruit and other missiles thrown at them. The omens were not good.

When the game began, Peter Bonetti accidentally clattered into a Roma player when clearing his goalmouth and the violent tone was set for the rest of the evening. Bonetti was bombarded with fruit and bottles as the atmosphere grew more menacing by the minute. If a Chelsea player went near the touchline, missiles were thrown at him. John Boyle was knocked out when an empty wine bottle smashed into his head. After a lengthy stoppage, Boyle resumed battle stations. An iron bar was then hurled in the direction of John Hollins and missed him only by inches. Eddie McCreadie was then felled by a bottle and he too was knocked unconscious. This was by far the most violent crowd behaviour that any British team had ever been subjected to.

In one of the bravest displays of courage of all time, Chelsea battled away and held Roma to a 0-0 draw. The team ran for their lives at the final whistle, eager to reach the relative safety of the dressing-rooms. Even then, Chelsea's torment was not over, with the team coach being attacked by someone wielding an iron bar as the Italian police stood by and did nothing. After an inquiry into the incidents Roma were found guilty of orchestrating the hate campaign against Chelsea, and were banned from all European competitions for three years. They were also fined a derisory £500. Chelsea boss Tommy Docherty was unimpressed, and remarked, 'They should have been closed down for good!'

COLLINS SUBJECTED TO SHEER THUGGERY

Torino 0–0 Leeds United
Inter-Cities Fairs Cup
6 October 1965

This was one of the most brutal games in Leeds United's history. After winning the first-leg tie at Elland Road 2-1, Leeds knew the Italians would throw everything at them in the return. The first game had been a physical encounter but Don Revie's team did not expect the sheer thuggery that was inflicted on them in Italy.

Leeds' midfield maestro and captain Bobby Collins had been singled out as the player that made Leeds tick and Torino decided to take him out of the game at the first possible opportunity. Poletti hit Collins with a tackle of such venom and force that his thigh bone was broken. The fact that Collins was ten yards from the ball when contact was made was immaterial to Poletti.

The Torino player went unpunished and Collins was stretchered off to be taken for hospital treatment. Billy Bremner, recalling the incident years later, said, 'I think that must have been the only time in history that anyone has broken his femur on a football field. It usually takes a tremendous impact, such as a car crash, to cause such an injury.'

Bremner and the rest of his Leeds teammates spent the rest of the game waiting for the opportunity to inflict painful retribution on Poletti. Fortunately for the Torino player, he managed to evade the Leeds team for the whole match, and a hard-fought 0-0 draw took the Yorkshire team through to the next round of the competition. Many, including his Leeds teammates, thought that Collins' career had been brought to an end there and then. But the tough little Scot did return and played professional football until 1973. Bremner later recalled: 'When I saw Bobby Collins lying there with his thigh bone broken, I began to cry. If I'd had the chance I would have crippled the player who did that to him.'

BIG JACK BLOWS HIS TOP

Leeds United 1-2 Valencia
Inter-Cities Fairs Cup
2 February 1966

Yet another violent encounter from Leeds United's adventures in what one soccer pundit suggested should be renamed the 'Not Fairs' Cup. This time, Leeds' opponents were Spanish team Valencia.

The Leeds team were no angels, but Valencia's display of body checking, hacking and shirt pulling surprised even them. The volatile Jack Charlton had been singled out by the Spanish for some extra special intimidatory treatment. As expected, Charlton, unable to contain himself any longer after being subjected to sly digs and kicks throughout the game, exploded and decided to dish out some punishment of his own.

After making his way into the Valencia penalty area to put in a challenge for a high cross, a Spanish player threw a punch at Charlton. Big Jack went berserk and chased after the Valencia goalkeeper who Charlton had singled out as the player that had aimed the punch at him. A mass brawl ensued and police ran on to the pitch in an attempt to restore order. The referee, Leo Horn, decided to take the two teams off the field of play in an attempt to calm them down. Word was then sent to the Leeds dressing-room that Jack Charlton had been sent off along with Valencia's Garcia Ridagany.

With order seemingly restored, the two teams restarted play with just fifteen minutes remaining. The violence did not end there, however. Sanchez Lage of Valencia decided to try to break Jim Storrie's leg with a scything tackle and he too was sent off. The game ended in a 1-1 draw, and after the game the referee told the press that he was surprised at Charlton's behaviour. 'I saw a Spanish defender kick Charlton and if Jack had given the Spaniard a reprisal kick I would have let it pass,' said Horn. 'Jack Charlton is a fine man but he lost all control.' Norman Hunter of Leeds described the sight of seeing Jack Charlton chasing the length of the pitch in pursuit of the Valencia goalkeeper as the funniest sight he ever saw in the whole of his career. Billy Bremner recalled the game thus:

> Valencia put on the worst show of hacking, shirt tugging and body checking I have ever seen. Jackie Charlton came in for the biggest hammering. It is understandable that he hit out and I would have done the same. Human endurance has to snap at some time.

Big Jack's take on it was:

> One of the Valencia players slung a punch at me that would have done credit to Cassius Clay (Mohammed Ali). I went berserk; I chased around the penalty area intent about getting my own back. I had completely lost control of myself after those diabolical fouls on me. Suddenly players seemed to be pushing and jostling each other. Police appeared on the field to stop this game of football degenerating into a running battle.

THE BUTCHERS OF BUENOS AIRES

England 1-0 Argentina
World Cup quarter-final
23 July 1966

'The butchers of Buenos Aires make football a farce,' proclaimed one newspaper headline after the game. England manager Alf Ramsey was so incensed by the Argentinian tactics that he ran on to the pitch at the end of the game to stop his team exchanging shirts with the South Americans. The England boss branded the Argentine team as 'animals' though he did apologise later for his remark. David Miller of *The Sunday Telegraph* said of the game, 'Football had been degraded beyond endurance by an Argentine team with cultured feet and kindergarten minds. Theirs is the law of the jungle. They are equally

accomplished in every art of the chop, hack, trip and body check.'
Hurst's glancing header thirteen minutes from the end gave England
a 1-0 win, but it was a victory that had to be fought for in a physical
as well as a footballing sense.

From the kick-off, Bobby Moore and his England team found
themselves under extreme provocation from a talented but cynical
Argentine team. Ten minutes from the interval, the game erupted
when Rattin, the Argentina captain, disputed the referee's decision
to book one of his teammates. Already with his name in the official's
notebook, Rattin's verbal abuse of the referee led to his dismissal from
the field of play. Rattin refused to go and at one stage it appeared that
his teammates were going to refuse to carry on with the game. After
ten minutes of arguing, Rattin reluctantly walked to the dressing-
room, running the gauntlet of England's baying supporters in the process. England were not entirely blameless for this dour game, conceding
just as many free-kicks as the Argentinians in an explosive first half.
Nobby Stiles was recently asked about the game and replied:

Referee Rudolf Kreitlein has to be escorted off the pitch by the police at
the end of the ill-tempered England *v.* Argentina 1966 World Cup clash.

If Argentina had concentrated on the football, they could have won the World Cup. They were a great side, but the things they were getting up to off the ball were unbelievable. The stuff they were doing was unreal. Today, with TV cameras everywhere, you wouldn't get away with it.

The great Bobby Moore, who led England to glory in the 1966 tournament did not have fond memories of the Argentina game either:

They were sure as hell not pleasant to play against. They did do nasty things. They did tug your hair, spat at you, poked you in the eyes and kicked you when the ball was miles away. Lads like Ballie, Nobby and Jack Charlton were getting steamed-up. I just said the only way to deal with them was to beat the bastards!

Dr Menendez Betly, president of the Argentine FA, said:

We do not approve of the conduct of our players and officials yesterday, but they were provoked by the referee. He was absolutely biased in favour of England. He was against Argentina from the start. Argentinians are not dirty players. They have never broken opponents' legs. Who was badly hurt in the England side?

The referee himself, Rudolf Kreitlein, said, 'I have refereed all over the world and this was undoubtedly the roughest game'. The final crime count at the end of the game was: (Argentina) one sent off, five booked; (England) two booked. The England players who found themselves in one ref's notebook were Jack and Bobby Charlton.

FERGUSON BURSTS BALL

Northern Ireland 0–2 England
European Championship qualifier
22 October 1966

Billy Ferguson became the first Irish player to be sent off in an international game and also the first to receive his marching orders in a Home International during this fiery encounter. The game took place in October 1966 at Windsor Park, Belfast. England were the newly crowned World Champions and they paraded the trophy before an enthusiastic 58,000 crowd before the kick-off.

When the game began it was soon clear that Northern Ireland were determined not to be overawed by their more illustrious opponents. The Irish, in fact, could boast an array of stars themselves, such as George Best, Derek Dougan and Pat Jennings. The game had the added spice of being not just another Home International, but also a qualifier for the 1968 European Championships. Qualification for the final stages depended on the combined results of the Home Internationals for the next two seasons.

As expected, George Best taunted the England defence from the start. His Manchester United teammate Nobby Stiles tried hard to keep Best under control, but at times it looked like Best might beat England single-handedly. As the tackles began to fly in, tempers began to fray. Nobby Stiles and Derek Dougan were booked by the referee for an incident at the start of the second half. Tired of the rough treatment that he was on the receiving end of, Best also became involved in some fiery tackles as both teams fought for superiority. England, who had taken the lead through Hunt just before the interval, clinched the game through a Martin Peters header in the second period. George Best was lucky to escape with a lecture after a vicious tackle on Alan Ball.

The game had been threatening to spiral out of control all afternoon and five minutes from the end the young Linfield forward Billy Ferguson made British football history. Ferguson hit Alan Ball with a brutal tackle that was deemed dangerous by the referee, R. Davidson of Scotland. Ferguson was stunned to be sent off when a booking was the most that he expected for his indiscretion. As he trooped off in front of his home supporters, Windsor Park being Linfield's home ground, he was probably totally unaware that he had secured his place in the record books for an achievement that was the last thing that he would have coveted. Billy Ferguson went on to make just one more international appearance, against Mexico in 1967.

THE BATTLE OF MONTEVIDEO

Racing Club 1-0 Celtic
World Club Championship
1 November 1967

The World Club Championship, which was first held in 1961, was contested by the winners of the European Cup and the winners of the South American Copa Libertadores. Jock Stein's Celtic were determined to become the first British winners of this trophy.

If there was a top ten of the most violent games of all time, this would have to be a strong contender for the number one spot. After a win for Celtic at Hampden Park, and then a Racing Club success in the return game in Buenos Aires, a decider was rapidly arranged to take place in Uruguay just three days later. The second game had been violent enough; Celtic goalkeeper Ronnie Simpson had been hit by a brick as he ran out for the kick-off, and was unable to take his place in goal. The third and final encounter was, however, an out-and-out brawl. Celtic, and in particular tricky winger Jimmy Johnstone, had been the victims of some harsh tackling in the Buenos Aires game, and they decided that they would get their retribution in first this time.

As expected, the tackling was fierce, and Johnstone was Racing Club's main target. Unable to contain himself any longer, having been subjected to a barrage of kicking and spitting during the first half of play, Johnstone was the first to be sent off when he elbowed a

Racing Club defender in the face. After that the game became utter carnage, with private vendettas being carried out in every area of the pitch. At times, the police had to intervene to stop the brawling players. John Hughes of Celtic was next to go for kicking the Racing Club goalkeeper. The referee, who earlier in the game had got the two captains together to warn them that the foul play had to stop, completely lost control of the game.

Bobby Lennox of Celtic also received his marching orders, along with two Racing Club players as the eight against nine men encounter degenerated into a farce. A fourth Celtic player was also dismissed from the field of play towards the end of the game, but in the general melee of violence and brawling that had now engulfed proceedings he decided not to go, and Celtic played on with eight men. When pictures of this sensational game were shown to a disbelieving world, the general feeling was that this was a competition that had no place in the sports arena.

Celtic's Bobby Murdock attempts to drag Racing Club's Gardenas off the pitch during the brutal 1967 match for the World Club Championship.

Uruguayan police with batons drawn attempt to keep the Celtic and Racing Club players apart during the incredible World Club Championship game between the South American and European Champions.

Racing Club took the trophy with a 1-0 victory but no one really cared. In the aftermath of the game an embarrassed Jock Stein fined his team for their behaviour. According to reports from Argentina, however, Racing Club rewarded their players by providing them with a new car each.

ALAN MULLERY MAKES HISTORY

Yugoslavia 1-0 England
5 June 1968
European Championships semi-final

In modern-day football sendings-off are commonplace, but unbelievably England did not have a player sent off in a full international game until 1968. The dubious honour of being the first went to Alan Mullery. Mullery was a hard, skilful midfielder who began his career at Fulham before moving to Spurs in 1964 for £72,500, a record fee for a British player.

Spurs already had one of the greatest midfield enforcers of the era, Dave Mackay, in their ranks, and Mullery was not quite in his league. Gradually though, the London-born wing-half won the fans over with his accomplished and competitive displays.

Alan Mullery was selected by Alf Ramsey for his England debut against Holland in 1965 but had to wait two years for his next cap, against Spain in 1967. The match against Spain was a European Championship quarter-final tie and Mullery performed well in place of Nobby Stiles to help England to a 1-0 victory. England won the away leg against Spain 3-1 to set up a semi-final against Yugoslavia. In their quarter-final Yugoslavia had beaten France 6-2 over two legs and were expected to be formidable opponents.

The semi-final took place in the Studio Communale, Florence. Alan Mullery retained his place in the team ahead of Nobby Stiles

Alan Mullery is a dejected figure as he trudges off after being dismissed against Yugoslavia in a 1968 European Championship game. He became the first England player in history to be sent off.

and the scene was set for a classic encounter between the reigning World Champions and one of Europe's up-and-coming international teams.

On the evening of the game the heat in the Florence stadium was unbearable. The Yugoslavian manager, Rajko Mitic, had caused a mild stir before the game when he told the press, 'I am determined to avoid individual physical duals because England have the greater physical ability.' Most of England's international opponents during this period would express concern about England's over-physical approach to the game.

In the first period of the match the tackles certainly flew in from both sets of players and neither side gave much away in terms goal-scoring opportunities. Bobby Charlton went close in the second half as the tackling became fiercer by the minute. With just four minutes remaining, Yugoslavia took the lead through Dzajic. With England desperate for an equaliser to take the game into extra time, Mullery pressed forward but had his foot stamped on by Trivic. The fiery Spurs midfielder chased after the fleeing Yugoslavia player to return the compliment and kicked his assailant on the back of his leg. Trivic hit the turf as though hit by a round of machine gun fire and Mullery knew his place in English football history had been sealed. The referee, ignoring Trivic's stamp on the England midfielder, sent Mullery off. He became the first England player to receive his marching orders. Yugoslavia held on to win the game and they met Italy in the final, which they lost 2-0 after a replay.

Mullery's dismissal was headline news in England. England boss Alf Ramsey stayed loyal to Mullery, saying, 'It would appear that you can kick a player in front of the referee and get away with it. Alan Mullery retaliated, the referee also saw it and he got sent off. It was a rough game.' The report in the *Daily Telegraph* read:

> It was a black day for the world champions in Florence. Alan Mullery was the culprit, kicking an opponent who had just hit him with a late tackle. Mullery, perhaps was paying for Norman Hunter's crippling tackle that put Osim out of what was a vicious game.

While according to The Times:

> It was a bruising, cynical encounter, culminating in the second-half with Mullery being sent off. Mullery had his excuses – he had been brought down with a late tackle by Trivic – but his retaliatory kick at the perpetrator, compounded by the forward's thespian display, left the referee with little choice.

NOBBY STILES EL BANDITO

Estudiantes de la Plata 1-0 Manchester United
World Club Championship
25 September 1968

Manchester United's game against the Argentine club Estudiantes, who were South American Champions, was a stormy affair from the off. The Buenos Aires press campaign to vilify United's tough tackling Nobby Stiles began well before the team had touched down on Argentinian soil. 'Stiles the Assassin' was a typical headline and when the United team took to the field for the opening leg, Nobby was introduced to the crowd over the tannoy as 'El Bandito'.

From the start, the United team were subjected to spitting, hair pulling and blatant intimidation. Bobby Charlton had to be carried off with a leg wound that needed stitches after only fifteen minutes' play. Nobby Stiles came in for special treatment and received a gash over his eye after a blatant headbutt by Bilardo. Matt Busby had told his players what to expect but had appealed to them not to retaliate. Pat Crerand recalled, 'If we were kicked or punched, we just had to take it. The boss made this quite clear.' Nobby Stiles also remembers Busby's pre-match instructions: 'Instead of saying "sod off", you had to be nice to them. Mind you, we never won when it was a rough house, we were never at our best.'

George Best was expected to be United's trump card, but even he had the heart kicked out of him after a dreadful early foul. After that Best quickly lost his appetite for the match.

GEORGE BEST LOSES HIS COOL

Manchester United 1-1 Estudiantes de la Plata
World Club Championship
16 October 1968

Manchester United were confident they could overturn Estudiantes' one-goal first-leg lead at Old Trafford, but a goal by Madero after only five minutes put the South Americans in firm control of the tie. Once again Denis Law and George Best were singled out for some appalling treatment but the general consensus was that the game was not as violent as the Buenos Aires game. Law had to go off just before the interval to have his leg stitched after the Estudiantes goalkeeper raked him with his studs. Best was subjected to the usual array of spitting, pinching, and other niggling tactics that led to him finally losing his cool after Medina spat in his face. Best responded by slapping his tormentor full in the face. The Argentinian collapsed to the turf and both players were sent off. Medina was keen to carry on the fight when he followed Best to the touchline, but was quickly ushered down the tunnel by officials. Speaking about the Estudiantes games in recent years, George remarked:

It was the biggest shock of my life. They would try and hurt you. They were not interested in playing football. It seemed their main idea was to get as many of our players off the pitch as possible. One player spent the entire two legs trying to kick me. They were out to stop me any way they could. In the home game, I finally snapped and smacked this bloke. I walked off before the ref sent me off. That was one time when I did react viciously.

Although Willie Morgan, United's best attacking player over the two legs, gave the Reds hope with a late goal, Estudiantes held out to take the cup. Some of the Argentinians stood on the touchline at the end of the game applauding the United players off, but the simmering resentment that they felt towards the Estudiantes team meant they were not in the mood for such gestures and Alex Stepney, the United goalkeeper, gave Oscar Pachame a backhander as he walked past him.

Always magnanimous in defeat, even defeats suffered under such acrimonious circumstances, Matt Busby refused to condemn the South Americans and told the press, 'Manchester United's players can hold their heads high. They lost like men. Like men we shall be trying again. Have no doubts about it. We shall go on and on, as we went on and on until we won the European Cup, and we will win this World Club Championship.'

THE GAME THAT STARTED A WAR

Honduras 2-3 El Salvador
World Cup qualifier
30 June 1969

From the inaugural World Cup held in Uruguay in 1930, through to modern-day World Cup games, violence has been a regular occurrence. In the 1930 tournament the opening game saw France take on Mexico. The match was only ten minutes old when the French goalkeeper had to be stretchered off with a broken jaw, courtesy of a flying boot from a Mexican attacker. Argentina, who were in the same group as France, kicked and conned their way to the final. Their opponents were host country Uruguay. The atmosphere surrounding the final resembled a war zone. Thousands of Argentinians travelled from Buenos Aires to Montevideo across the River Plate. The Argentinian fans marched through the streets chanting 'victory or death' as they made their way to the stadium. Uruguayan soldiers with fixed bayonets searched the marauding mob for knives and firearms. Uruguay went on to win the first ever World Cup, a result which did not go down at all well back in Argentina. Police had to open fire on disgruntled Argentinian fans who laid siege to the Uruguayan Embassy in Buenos Aires.

If the first World Cup came close to starting a war between two South American countries, some claim that a 1969 World Cup qualifier between Honduras and El Salvador was the catalyst for a violent conflict between the two countries. After two semi-final games between these neighbouring countries, who were competing for a place in the match that would determine who out of Central and North America would qualify for the 1970 World Cup Finals, a third play-off match was arranged. The game took place in Mexico and El Salvador were the victors by a 3-2 scoreline.

There had been crowd trouble at all three games and relations between the two countries were not in a healthy state. Fighting had been taking place for months on the borders that divided the two countries. There were claims by Honduras that their country was being overrun by workers from El Salvador seeking employment. El Salvador's victory in the World Cup qualifier was the final straw for Honduras and hostilities between the countries began in earnest.

Just two weeks after the game, El Salvador launched a bombing campaign on Honduras, with many casualties suffered by both sides. Honduras retaliated by invading El Salvador and the final death count in the conflict was put at over 2,000.

OUT-AND-OUT WAR

Leeds United 1-2 Chelsea
FA Cup final replay
29 April 1970

This 1970 FA Cup final replay between Leeds and Chelsea at Old Trafford was recently described by Chelsea's John Hollins as 'a brutal, violent, no holds barred, pitched battle'. The first game at Wembley was a typical hard-fought game with Chelsea matching Leeds for aggression every inch of the way. It was the replay that ensured that the game would go down in history as the most violent FA Cup final ever. Recalling the game, Chelsea forward Ian Hutchinson once said, 'If you didn't compete with Leeds you would get kicked off the park. So you geed yourself up before you went out. It was out-and-out-war.'

The tone was set for the Old Trafford replay during the first few minutes when Ron 'Chopper' Harris, who had been switched to right-back in a bid to stop the player who had run Chelsea ragged in the first game, Eddie Gray, went through on the Leeds winger with a thunderous tackle. It was rumoured that Harris hit Gray so high that the Chelsea hard man's studs had traces of the winger's shorts on them. After this, Gray did not dare to torment Chelsea the way he had in the wide open spaces of Wembley.

The tackles continued to fly in and McCreadie hit Bremner with a waist-high challenge and Hunter and Hutchinson became embroiled in a stand-up fight with the play taking place at the other end of the pitch. The lenient referee decided against taking action against any of the players as the bone-crunching tackling continued unabated. Chelsea goalkeeper Bonetti was also knocked unconscious during the first half when Jones clattered into him. Minutes later, the still-dazed Bonetti was beaten by Jones to give Leeds the lead.

Although Leeds had had by far the better of the football action that did take place, Chelsea kept them to just a one-goal advantage and sneaked an equaliser when Peter Osgood ran on to a Charlie Cooke pass to head the ball past the Leeds goalkeeper. During extra time it was David Webb who scored an unlikely winner for the resilient Chelsea team, who had matched Leeds blow for blow and kick for kick in the roughest FA Cup final of all time. In effect, they had out-Leedsed Leeds.

Ron 'Chopper' Harris of Chelsea said, 'There are a few brave players around. Players that I look at and think, "he's as tough as me!" Norman Hunter and Billy Bremner at Leeds are two of the toughest.' Bremner once gave an insight into why Leeds were such a tough side, saying, 'At Leeds every player is taught to put side before self. Above my peg in the dressing-room there hangs a motto: "Always keep on fighting." That means exactly what it says. You keep fighting for the whole team, not just yourself.'

Of the game, John Giles said:

> The replay at Old Trafford was spoiled by tackling in the x-certificate class! I expected this. Old Trafford with its more enclosed, intense atmosphere made our clash with Chelsea more like a semi-final than a final. There is bound to be the odd flash of needle between hard tackling, determined teams like Leeds and Chelsea.

FISTICUFFS OVER DINNER

Lazio 2–2 Arsenal
European Fairs Cup
16 September 1970

The sensational goings-on at Old Trafford in October 2004, which have now gone down in history as 'The Battle of the Buffet', were not the first time that the lads from Highbury had been involved in a food fight. In September 1970, Arsenal, the reigning European Fairs Cup holders, were drawn to play Italian club Lazio in the first round of the competition. They travelled to Rome for the first leg and were fully aware that the Italians, apart from being capable of playing good football, could also dish out the physical stuff if they were in the mood. However, the Arsenal team of this period had its fair share of hard men, such as Storey, Rice, McLintock, Radford and Kennedy. If the game turned into a rough-house they were prepared for it.

The game itself turned out to be the anticipated physical encounter, but despite being on the receiving end of some brutal tackles and the usual provocation that British teams encountered abroad, Arsenal retained their composure. John Radford netted twice to give the London club a 2-2 draw. All appeared well after the game and the Arsenal team prepared themselves for an after-match meal courtesy of their Italian hosts. The idea of the two opposing teams joining up for food and alcoholic drinks after a game probably seems quite alien to modern-day football fans, but this was quite common on European trips in the 1960s and '70s. The meal appeared to be quite a cordial affair, then at some point in the evening, Lazio players felt that they were being accused of misdemeanours that they were supposed to have committed during the game by some of the Arsenal team.

What happened next is still unclear to this day. Some reports claim that Ray Kennedy was attacked by a Lazio player and then a full-scale brawl erupted. The fight spilled out into the street before order was restored. Arsenal goalkeeper Bob Wilson gave his account of events:

> After the game, a restaurant near the centre of Rome hosted a reception for both teams. There was a hostile atmosphere. Late at night I heard heated exchanges between Ray Kennedy and some Italians. Within seconds Ray was attacked and a fight started. Bertie Mee could be seen pulling players away. Only the arrival of local police on two motorbikes subdued the fighting.

No reporters witnessed the fisticuffs so it is hard to ascertain what exactly instigated the flare-up. All that Arsenal boss Bertie Mee would say about the affair when the team arrived back in London was that he was looking forward to the return leg at Highbury. There was even speculation that the second leg might be called off, but Mee commented, 'I feel the matter is best forgotten as quickly as possible and I don't intend getting drawn into any controversy by commenting on what happened. We will be happy to receive Lazio at Highbury on Wednesday and they will receive all the normal Highbury hospitality.' When pushed about the brawl, Mee admitted, 'One or two of my players do have minor cuts and bruises and we did receive a lot of provocation during the match. I felt that had a lot to do with what happened later.'

Lazio were adamant that they were not at fault. Dr Giambartolemie, a club director, did admit however that perhaps they provided just a little too much vino: 'One could largely say that it was our fault because with the dinner we provided some excellent wine.' But Giambartolemie did ask for an apology for remarks directed at Lazio players. He said, 'Arsenal should make it clear that no insult was intended by these comments and that the incident was merely due to an excess of conviviality. We also want a guarantee that next Wednesday we will be able to play football and not a bull-fight.'

The return leg at Highbury did not turn out to be the bloodbath that many expected and Arsenal won the game quite comfortably 2-0. After a UEFA inquiry into the brawl in Rome Lazio received a fine, with no action taken against Arsenal for their part in it.

PANDEMONIUM AT ELLAND ROAD

Leeds United 1-2 West Bromwich Albion
17 April 1971

The 1970/71 season was a strange affair for Leeds United. They were knocked out of the FA Cup 3-2 in a sensational game against Fourth Division Colchester United; they tasted triumph in Europe, winning the Inter-Cities Fairs Cup, beating Juventus on the away-goals rule over two legs in the final; but in the battle for the League title Leeds fans to this day claim that they were robbed.

The source of their grievance was the 17 April 1971 fixture against West Bromwich Albion. The Midlands club were relatively safe from the threat of relegation, just below mid-table in the League, but Leeds were fighting tooth and nail for the title. Leeds started the day two points clear of Arsenal, but the London club had played two fewer games. Leeds needed victory to maintain their title push.

A group of incensed Leeds players have to be restrained from manhandling referee Ray Tinker after he allowed West Bromwich Albion's hotly disputed second goal to stand.

From the kick-off Leeds pushed forward for an early goal, but it was West Brom who took a shock lead through Tony Brown after twenty minutes. The second half followed the same pattern as the first with all the pressure coming from Leeds but Albion dangerous on the break. The dramatic passage of action that sent the Elland Road crowd and the Leeds team into a violent frenzy came with twenty-eight minutes still to play. West Brom's Tony Brown intercepted a Hunter pass and the ball rebounded into the Leeds half. Albion's Colin Suggett pursued the loose ball with Brown, but the linesman flagged for offside against Suggett.

Unbelievably the referee Ray Tinkler allowed play to continue as the Leeds defence stood still expecting an offside decision to be given. West Brom played on and Brown passed to Jeff Astle, who also looked offside, who sidefooted the ball past Gary Sprake in the Leeds goal. When the goal was scored there was hardly a Leeds player in his own half. The Leeds players went crazy and irate Leeds supporters began to invade the playing area. One of the linesmen was hit by a missile and the Leeds players themselves had to protect the referee from the rioting fans as police fought to restore order. Many spectators were arrested as the pitch was eventually cleared. The game was restarted and, although Leeds pulled a goal back through Clarke, West Brom held on for a controversial victory.

The game was something of a sensation when shown on television that evening. Don Revie, the Leeds manager, and his players had no doubts that they had been the victims of a great injustice, but the referee, Ray Tinkler, was adamant that Suggett was not interfering with play during the build-up to Albion's second goal.

Don Revie and the board of directors at Leeds lodged a protest to the Football League about the referee's handling of the game. Television replays showed that the linesman originally did raise his flag for offside against Suggett, but then decided to put it down again. Even the West Brom boss, Alan Ashman, agreed that the goal was offside, but the result stood and Arsenal went on to win the League title by one point from Leeds.

After an FA inquiry into the Elland Road riot, Leeds were fined £750 and ordered to play their first four home games of the following season on a neutral ground. Despite these FA sanctions against Leeds, there were still rather strange comments coming out of Elland Road that appeared to vindicate the rioting crowd's behaviour. Don Revie remarked, 'I don't blame them at all. The referee's decision in allowing the goal was diabolical.' Leeds' chairman, Percy Woodward, was reported as saying, 'I am not blaming the spectators. There was every justification for it.'

THE BATTLE OF BARCELONA

Rangers 3–2 Moscow Dynamo
European Cup-Winners' Cup final
23 May 1972

This should have been one of Glasgow Rangers' finest moments. Just a year after the Ibrox disaster, when a crush at one of the stairways leading from the ground resulted in the tragic death of sixty-six supporters, Rangers fought their way to the final of the 1972 European Cup-Winners' Cup. Their opponents were Moscow Dynamo and the game took place in Barcelona. It was estimated that 20,000 Rangers fans had flown from Glasgow to support their team. Before the match had even begun one Rangers fan found himself in hospital with a fractured skull after falling from his hotel window. It was also reported that over 100 fans went on a drunken spree in Lloret de Mar and smashed up a bar.

The match itself was not a particularly violent affair and Rangers, through goals by Colin Stein and two by Willie Johnston, were 3–0 up with forty minutes still to play. The problem was that after each goal there was a pitch invasion by jubilant Rangers fans who wanted to celebrate each goal with the players. There had been warnings by loudspeakers before the game that pitch invasions would not be tolerated. At first the local Spanish police took a softly softly approach to the pitch invasions, but near the end of the game the atmosphere turned distinctly hostile. With Rangers hanging on to a 3–2 lead, their supporters thought that the referee had blown for full-time. This was the signal for yet another pitch invasion, but this time the police began to wade into the Scots with their batons.

The Rangers fans fought back with bottles and pieces of wood ripped from the stands. One of the Moscow players was hit over the head with a bottle in the general melee that now engulfed the playing area. The match officials and the two teams fled the riotous scenes as a full-scale battle erupted on the pitch. There was one killed and 150 injured as Rangers fans and the police waded into each other.

The violence spilled over into the streets surrounding the ground and many Rangers fans were arrested and thrown into jail. After their great victory, the Rangers team had to be presented with the trophy in one of the rooms inside the stadium. A lap of honour was, understandably, out of the question.

The following day the clean-up of Barcelona's ground and the streets outside the stadium began. The eight bars inside the stadium had been smashed up during the fighting. Moscow Dynamo appealed to UEFA for the result to be declared void, but this was rejected. The president of UEFA, Gustav Wiederkehr, said, 'The Scottish fans behaved like savages. We must find a way to keep such people from the stadiums.'

Although the result was allowed to stand, Rangers were banned from all European competition for two years. This was later reduced

An injured Rangers fan is helped off after being injured during the massive pitch invasion that led to a full-scale riot at the end of the Glasgow club's 1972 European Cup-Winners' Cup final against Moscow Dynamo.

to one year. When the Rangers team arrived back in Glasgow they were given a fantastic reception when they displayed the trophy at Ibrox Park. One of the Rangers supporters, a Glasgow police sergeant, blamed the trouble on the Spanish police. 'The police allowed the fans on to the pitch and then attacked them with batons. The Spanish police were a cowardly atrocious bunch.' However, John Mains, Lord Provost of Glasgow, remarked, 'The hooligan element amongst the fans have brought disgrace to Glasgow and Scotland.'

THE DAY CHARLIE CUT CHOPPER DOWN TO SIZE

Arsenal 1-1 Chelsea
2 September 1972

Coming just a few days after a home victory over West Ham United, Arsenal were looking to confirm their position as London's number one team. Chelsea, who had ambitions of their own, were determined to make Arsenal fight every inch of the way for the points. As expected, the tackles flew in thick and fast as the game took on an air of brutality from the start.

Chelsea's Ron 'Chopper' Harris and Arsenal's Peter Storey were determined to come out on top in the battle for the title of London's premier hard man. But, as it turned out, it was to be a long-haired forward who would have the press baying for his blood at the end of the game.

Coming on as a substitute for George Armstrong, Charlie George set about playing Ron Harris at his own game. Harris hit George, who had only been on the field a few minutes, with a pile-driver of a tackle, but fell to the turf himself in the process. Charlie George then got to his feet and proceeded to jump up and down on Harris's chest. A mass brawl then ensued before order was restored.

The game was played out in an atmosphere of impending violence, but nobody was sent off despite the ferocity of the tackling.

Honours were even as both teams took a point in a 1-1 draw. But in the aftermath of the game there was mass condemnation of Charlie George for his treatment of Harris. 'Chopper' himself did not complain and said that as far as he was concerned the matter was closed. Arsenal chairman Dennis Hill-Wood told the press, 'Charlie was sinned against, sinned himself, and was then sinned against again.' But Harris's Chelsea teammates were not happy with George's behaviour, and a statement was issued that read, 'If George persists in hurting other professionals he will eventually be taken on by someone who is bigger and stronger.'

Charlie George himself recently talked about the infamous 1972 Arsenal *v.* Chelsea derby and said, 'Every time I played against 'Chopper' I took a right hammering. But I gave as good as I got. Ron whacked me really hard during that game, so I jumped up and down on his chest. He was coughing up blood, according to the papers. I remember everyone then piled in and it was a mass brawl.'

HUNTER BECOMES THE HUNTED

Leeds United 0-1 AC Milan
European Cup Winners' Cup final
16 May 1973

Battle-weary Leeds, who had finished third to Liverpool in the championship race, and then lost to Sunderland in the greatest FA Cup final upset of our time, were desperate to end the season with at least one trophy to their name. The final of the European Cup-Winners' Cup took place against AC Milan in Salonika, Greece. From the outset Milan went in hard and, backed by some dubious refereeing decisions, looked as determined as their English rivals to take the trophy. Leeds, who had by far the better of the play, came up against an inspired goalkeeper in Milan's Vecchi and could not make a breakthrough.

A rather fortuitous goal by Chiarugi – a shot that took several deflections on its way into the net – gave Milan the lead and from then on Leeds laid siege to the Italian goal. A mixture of solid defending and cynical tackling kept Leeds at bay as they frantically searched for an equaliser. 'They were trying to maim some of our players,' recalled Billy Bremner, as first Jones and then Lorimer became the victims of limb-threatening tackles.

The Greek crowd was by this time firmly behind the Yorkshire team as they drove forward to try and save the match. The action, which had been simmering for some time, finally exploded into violence when Norman Hunter was poleaxed by a Rivera foul. Hunter hit back and in the skirmish that followed Hunter and Sogliano exchanged blows and were both sent off.

Appeals for a blatant handball in the box by a Milan player were turned down near the end of the game and the Italians held on for a dubious 1-0 victory. The incensed Greek fans booed Milan as they tried to celebrate after the game and even struck up a chant of 'Shame, shame' as they paraded around the pitch. This was one occasion when Leeds, the team everyone loved to hate, were themselves the victims of an injustice.

VIOLENCE IN POLAND

Poland 3-0 Wales
World Cup Qualifier
26 September 1973

Bearded midfield terrier, Trevor Hockey, one of the stalwarts of the Wales team in the 1970s, found himself in the record books after this violent encounter. Hockey became the first Welsh international to be sent off when he was dismissed just before the half-time break. One newspaper described the game as 'A nightmare of delinquency. The spectacle was one of scything tackles from all directions – most of them I regret to say from men in the unaccustomed green shirt instead of the crimson strip of Wales.'

Trouble began as early as the seventh minute when Roberts hit a Polish player with a fierce tackle. Roberts had his name taken but the violence, from both Poland and Wales, did not end there. Hockey and Kasperczak exchanged blows in a midfield skirmish, but the referee decided to let the two players off with a lecture. While the free-kick was being taken, Hockey again became involved in a flare-up with Kasperczak and this time the referee sent him off.

With Wales two goals down, the second half became a desperate battle to avoid elimination from the World Cup. Brawls began to

Trevor Hockey in the colours of Aston Villa during the 1970s. Hockey might have looked like a hippy, but he was one of the most competitive midfield players in Britain during the sixties and seventies. He hit the headlines during the Wales *v*. Poland game in 1973 by becoming the first Wales player to be sent off playing for his country.

break out at regular intervals and Leighton James, one of the few not to become involved in the violence, was even attacked after offering a hand of apology to a Polish player after a clumsy challenge. Musial of Poland was then left writhing on the ground after becoming another victim of the reckless brutality on view. The crude challenges continued unabated until the end of the game, but the lenient Swedish referee was reluctant to stamp his authority on the game by sending any more players off. Poland scored again near the end to record a comfortable 3-0 victory.

LEN SHACKLETON
PREDICTS A RIOT

Newcastle United 4-3 Nottingham Forest
FA Cup quarter-final
9 March 1974

The 1970s was a decade when pitch invasions and violence on and off the playing area were quite common. Violence was not just confined to the English game. In 1974 alone, games in Spain and Greece had to be abandoned after gunshots were fired at match officials. Italy was a hotbed of soccer thuggery too and Scottish football also had its fair share of crowd disorder as the whole of Europe appeared to be caught up in a whirlpool of football mayhem.

In an age when violence at football matches was almost a weekly occurrence, it took something special for a sporting event to grab the attention of the nation. On 9 March 1974 the crowd at St James' Park really excelled themselves with a classic example of crowd disorder at a football match in the 1970s. The words of footballer Len Shackleton proved to be prophetic when he said the day before the match, 'I feel that there will be an uprising on Tyneside if Newcastle don't reach Wembley this year.'

The game began with Newcastle, who were comfortably placed in the First Division, expected to see off Second Division Nottingham Forest with few problems. Newcastle, in fact, were fancied to make it all the way to Wembley by many football pundits. The 54,000 crowd packed into St James' Park had come to see their boys brush Forest aside with ease, but it was the Midlands club who took control of the game from the start. Ian Bowyer put them ahead in the first minutes of the game and, although Newcastle drew level, Forest's O'Kane put them back in front just before the interval.

In the second half Forest looked to have built themselves an unassailable lead when Lyall put them 3-1 ahead from the penalty spot. Newcastle, apart from conceding another goal, looked to be really down and out when Howard was sent off for arguing with the referee about the penalty decision. Howard's dismissal was the signal for hundreds of spectators to invade the pitch. Faced with elimination from the FA Cup, St James' Park erupted. The initial invaders came from the Leazes End, where most of the young Newcastle fans congregated. *The Times'* football correspondent describing the pitch invasion reported that:

> Suddenly hundreds of Leazes Enders were on the field charging mindlessly around. They were set a dreadful example by a fat middle aged man who seemed determined to take on the Newcastle police force single handed. The referee wisely decided to take the teams off, but not, apparently, before two Forest players were assaulted.

When the police managed to clear the pitch, with the help of dogs, the game was restarted. From the restart, however, Forest appeared to be a totally different team. The ten men of Newcastle scored three goals in the last twenty minutes to win an incredible game. The break in play had certainly knocked Forest out of their stride. Nottingham Forest club officials, as well as the country at large, felt that the Second Division club had been cheated out of a famous victory by the hooligan element at St James' Park.

The casualty toll from the riot was twenty-three taken to hospital for treatment, two with fractured skulls, and over 100 treated at the ground for minor injuries. David Serella, the Forest defender, was one of two players punched and kicked by spectators. Serella accompanied the Nottingham Forest officials to an FA commission and after hearing all the evidence, the FA decided that the game should be replayed on a neutral ground. Nottingham Forest were delighted and their captain, R. Chapman (Sammy), told the press, 'We would have won it fair and square but for the trouble.'

The replay took place at Goodison Park. The first game resulted in a 0-0 draw. Three days later another replay finally saw Newcastle win through to the FA Cup semi-finals. Malcolm Macdonald scored United's goal in a 1-0 victory.

Newcastle eventually reached Wembley, but were soundly beaten by Bill Shankly's Liverpool in the 1974 final. Liverpool's 3-0 victory was taken by Nottingham Forest supporters, along with most of the nation's football followers, as justice being done.

Note: With the Newcastle riot making all the headlines on 9 March 1974, it is often overlooked that another sensational game took place just a day later. Plymouth Argyle had three players sent off in a violent encounter with Port Vale. Argyle were already down to ten men when, in injury time, referee Kevin McNally sent off David Provan and Bobby Saxton for violent conduct.

THE BATTLE OF MAINE ROAD

Manchester City 0–0 Manchester United
13 March 1974

Over the years the Manchester derby has thrown up some brutal encounters, but this was one of the worst. The 1973/74 season had been a disaster for one of English football's great clubs, Manchester

United. With Tommy Docherty at the helm, United found them-selves in the unlikely position of relegation candidates. When they visited their local neighbours, Manchester City, it was imperative that they got at least a point out of the game.

As expected, the opening minutes were white-hot with tackles flying in from all quarters. Mike Summerbee put Manchester United's Martin out of the game early on. The City winger, who, along with Everton's Johnny Morrissey, was the scourge of First Division full-backs in the 1960s and '70s, believed in getting his retaliation in first. Summerbee's foul on Martin earned him a booking and caused the United defender to exit the game, clutching his shoulder.

The United central defender Jim Holton was next to be booked for arguing with the referee. Little football was being played, with the game constantly being held up for free-kicks and players receiving treatment for injuries. It was inevitable that the match was going to explode at any moment and when Lou Macari and Mike Doyle became embroiled in a skirmish in the middle of the pitch, the referee decided to dispatch Macari and Doyle to the dressing-room for an early bath. Doyle began to walk off, but Macari refused to go. Doyle also then had second thoughts and began to question the referee about his involvement in the bust-up with Macari. With neither looking likely to budge, Clive Thomas then decided that the only course of action open to him was to take the two teams off the field of play. With the mood of the spectators growing uglier by the second, the bemused sets of players did as they were told and trouped down the tunnel. Five minutes later, both teams returned to the pitch, minus Macari and Doyle.

For the remainder of the game the atmosphere was still hostile and Forsyth was booked for a violent tackle. Other players from both sides were lucky to escape the referee's notebook as they both pushed forward for a winner. The game ended in a 0-0 draw and United knew that their chances of escaping the dreaded drop into the Second Division were hanging by a thread.

By a strange twist of fate, Manchester United did suffer the humiliating experience of losing their place in the First Division against Manchester City in the final game of the season. A goal from former United idol Denis Law saw them drop into the Second Division for the first time in thirty-five years. Law's goal in the eighty-second minute of the game was greeted by a mass pitch invasion and, on police advice, the referee abandoned the game. The result was allowed to stand and United started the 1974/75 campaign as a Second Division club.

FOOTBALL ARMAGEDDON

Celtic 0–0 Atletico Madrid
European Cup semi-final
9 April 1974

'This was not football, it was Armageddon, a sick nightmare which will become an infamous scar on the game in these islands,' reported Geoffrey Green of *The Times*. At the end of the game, the tally was nine bookings and three sent off. Atletico were managed by Juan Carlos Lorenzo, who had been in charge of the 1966 Argentina World Cup team that Alf Ramsey described as 'animals'. Lorenzo's Spanish Champions were certainly determined to return to Spain in a strong position to reach the European Cup final and were prepared to do literally anything to bring about the desired result.

The 73,000 that crammed into Parkhead roared their disapproval at the cynical tactics employed by the Spaniards, whose armoury contained every violent trick in the book. Celtic's brave winger Jimmy Johnsone suffered the most severe punishment as he was hacked down relentlessly every time he ran at the Atletico defence. A young Kenny Dalglish was playing that night and was horrified at what went on. Dalglish recalled, 'They were kicking us, trying to stop us anyhow. I got kicked but was treated lightly compared to Jimmy Johnstone. They considered Jimmy to be the most dangerous opponent. It was a horrible occasion.'

Eventually the Turkish referee had seen enough and began to take action. In the space of seventeen minutes, Ayala, Diaz and Quique were sent off for violent conduct. For the remainder of the game, Atletico played with eight in the penalty area as Celtic tried to batter them into submission. The Spanish held out for the draw they were determined to obtain at all costs. At the final whistle, Jimmy Johnstone was then attacked by a group of Atletico players and a free-for-all broke out.

Punches and kicks were aimed indiscriminately at each other by the two teams, and order was only restored when a large contingent of Glasgow police forced the two teams towards their respective dressing-rooms. A UEFA inquiry resulted in a £14,000 fine for Atletico but they went on to reach the final after a 2-0 home-leg win over their Glasgow opponents.

THE DAY KEVIN KEEGAN'S DAD NEARLY THUMPED BILLY BREMNER

Liverpool 1-1 Leeds United
FA Charity Shield
10 August 1974

After being sent off for fighting with Billy Bremner during the 1974 Charity Shield game, Kevin Keegan sat alone in the dressing-room at Wembley contemplating the enormity of what had just occurred. They had just become the first British players to be dismissed at the home of English football. Keegan, recalled the incident in his autobiography:

> I was sitting there shell-shocked when my dad came in. As he consoled me, Billy Bremner appeared. That was like a red rag to a bull as far as dad was concerned. He wanted to put one on Billy,

Two of the greatest players of their generation, Billy Bremner and Kevin Keegan, receive their marching orders from referee Bob Matthewson after exchanging blows during the 1974 Charity Shield game at Wembley between Leeds and Liverpool.

but Billy himself was very upset about the whole incident and we shook hands and apologised. I was devastated.

Keegan and Bremner, as well as being two of British football's greatest players, were both fiery characters on the field of play. If there was going to be a flare-up it was highly likely that Bremner and Keegan would be involved.

This was the first Charity Shield game played at Wembley, and it was also televised live. Right from the kick-off, the two best teams in the country at the time were determined that there would be little charity on display as the tackles flew in. Spectators and viewers could not believe their eyes as Leeds and Liverpool players hit each other with ferocious tackles. This was supposed to be a friendly curtain-raiser to the new season, but it was far from it. Leeds' Allan Clarke inflicted a nasty gash on Phil Thompson's leg with a nasty challenge as early as the tenth minute. The tone was now set for the rest of the game as Thompson's teammates looked for retribution. Inevitably it was Liverpool's chief enforcer, Tommy Smith, who caught up with Clarke first. After scything the Leeds striker down, Smith was booked by the referee. Then, during a brief interval when the football took over from the violence, Phil Boersma put Liverpool ahead.

It was during the second half that the game really erupted. Leeds' Johnny Giles was moving through on the Liverpool goal with Kevin Keegan clipping at his heels. Giles turned around and punched Keegan, but the lenient referee only booked Giles for what was clearly a sending-off offence. Two minutes later, however, referee Bob Matthewson was left with no other option when Billy Bremner and Kevin Keegan swapped punches. Once again, Johnny Giles was the instigator when he caught Keegan with a brutal tackle. Bremner told Keegan that he was play acting so the Liverpool star thumped him. Bremner hit back before their teammates split them up. After being sent off, the warring duo then took their shirts off and threw them down onto the ground. Strangely enough, this display of petulance caused almost as much of an uproar as their punch-up.

When the game continued, Trevor Cherry equalised for Leeds, but Liverpool took the trophy on penalties. The repercussions of Keegan and Brenner's flare-up reverberated throughout the nation for weeks afterwards. Newspapers branded the affair as 'Wembley's Day of Shame'. The FA, as expected, threw the book at Keegan and Bremner. Both were banned for eleven games and fined £500 each after the most brutal FA Charity Shield encounter of all time.

FIGHT OF THE CENTURY: FRANCIS LEE v. NORMAN HUNTER

Derby 3–2 Leeds
1 November 1975

To viewers of *Match of the Day* in 1975, this was one of the highlights of the season. Norman 'bites yer legs' Hunter's punch-up with Francis Lee. Even in the hard-tackling, anything-goes days of 1960s and '70s, this was sensational stuff. Lee had such a reputation as a master of the dive in the penalty area to obtain a penalty that even Joe Mercer, Lee's boss at Manchester City in the 1960s, nicknamed him 'ten-a-penno'. 'Francis would get us at least ten a season,' Joe would claim with a glint in his eye. Reigning champions Derby's match with Leeds in 1975 was to be yet another occasion when 'ten-a-penno' would win another dubious penalty for his team. But this time be was made to pay with stitches needed to sew his lip back together.

A full-blooded encounter between two of the best teams of the period came to the boil when Lee dashed into the penalty area to run on to a through bail from Charlie George. Hunter chased after him but did not appear to make much contact with Lee who was suddenly sprawling on the wet turf. The referee fell for Lee's three-card trick and George scored with the penalty. Hunter was furious, especially when Lee ran past him with a broad grin on his face.

Ten minutes into the second half, Norman Hunter, who had been biding his time waiting for the first opportunity to wipe the smirk off Lee's face, clattered into the Derby forward. A flurry of punches from both men followed and the referee sent them both off. As they made their way from the pitch, more comments were exchanged and a stand-up fight ensued. This time, Hunter managed to land the blow that split Lee's lip and the Derby forward required stitches to stem the flow of blood from the wound. By this stage players from both sides had also been involved in a mass brawl in the centre of the pitch.

Leeds boss Jimmy Armfield said after the game, 'I don't know what the solution is to an incident like that on Saturday. I have never seen Norman strike anyone before.'

WILLIE JOHNSTON KICKS THE REF UP THE ARSE

West Bromwich Albion 0–2 Brighton & Hove Albion
Football League Cup
22 September 1976

Once upon a time English football was littered with mavericks. Every top team seemed to have at least one player who possessed outstanding skills and who could change the course of a game with one piece of magic. The golden age for the football maverick was the 1960s and '70s. Since that time it has, in the main, all been downhill for those who appreciate watching footballers who have the ability to come up with the unexpected.

Recent decades have thrown up the odd player who possessed the ability to come up with something different, like Le Tissier, Gascoigne, Zola and their present-day equivalents Rooney and Ronaldinho, but they are few and far between. Most modern-day footballers are super-fit athletes who can run all day, but very few look like they are enjoying the game. Thank God for Ronaldinho, who actually plays the game with a smile on his face.

One of the greatest of the 1970s football mavericks was Willie Johnston. Johnston's greatest days were in the colours of Glasgow Rangers and in the 1971 European Cup-Winners' Cup final he almost single-handedly won the game for them with two brilliant goals. It was estimated that Johnston was sent off twenty-one times during his career, despite playing on the wing! The Rangers fans loved him and were disappointed to see him sign for West Bromwich Albion in 1972.

The English game didn't really see the best of Willie Johnston, who possessed devastating ability when in the mood. At Rangers, Johnston had received five red cards for punching opponents, usually in retaliation after being on the receiving end of a brutal tackle. At West Brom the same pattern followed, with two red cards in the 1973/74 season, one in the 1974/75 campaign and, most famously of all, his unique sending off in 1976 for kicking the referee up the backside. Johnston was always great entertainment, but Albion boss Don Howe must have sometimes asked himself if the £135,000 fee that the Midlands team paid for the cavalier winger was money well spent.

After winning promotion from the Second Division in 1976, West Bromwich Albion were going well in the top division at the start of the 1976/77 campaign. The Football League Cup was exactly the type of competition that Don Howe expected to do well in. When they were drawn against Third Division Brighton & Hove Albion, West Brom expected a comfortable ride into the fourth round of the competition, but it was Brighton who took the early initiative and Peter Ward shot them into the lead after four minutes. West Brom tried to raise their game, but Ward struck again on the half-hour and put Brighton 2-0 up.

The second half saw West Brom laying siege to the Brighton goal in an attempt to get back into the game. Willie Johnston felt that he was on the receiving end of some harsh treatment from the Brighton defenders and protested to the referee about the lack of protection he was getting from the officials. Two minutes from the end of the game and with the Baggies showing no signs of pulling back the two-goal deficit, Johnston was again hacked down. When the referee ignored his pleas for more protection, he decided to show Derek Lloyd how it felt to be on the receiving end of a kick and booted the startled official up the backside.

The players and supporters in the ground could not believe what they had just witnessed. Willie Johnston had been sent off in sensational circumstances during his career, but this was the most bizarre of the lot. Johnston was instantly dispatched to the dressing room and Brighton held on for a 2-0 victory.

The FA disciplinary committee held an inquiry into Willie Johnston's misdemeanour and rather leniently handed him just a five-match ban and £100 fine for bringing the game into disrepute. The committee said in a statement, 'If Johnston had deliberately intended an attack on the referee his right foot would not have missed the target.'

Johnston himself in later years admitted that he did aim a kick at him – 'Not to deliberately assault him, but to show him how it felt to suffer that sort of treatment. It was sheer frustration.' Johnston concluded, 'I must confess this one was bad, even considering the brutality I had suffered before I hit back.'

The FA's decision that Johnston's foot had only grazed Derek Lloyd's backside probably saved the Scottish star from a lengthy, if not lifetime, ban from the English game. He might have been unpredictable, but in a way it is sad that there are no players like Willie Johnston in the game today. Former Liverpool and England star Phil Neal described him thus:

> Willie Johnston had tremendous ability, he was skilful and quick but so easily riled. Then he became an animal. He would make wild lunges at you not caring whether he caught you or the ball, and his elbows would be everywhere. If ever a man had a reputation as one of football's bad boys, it was Willie and the referees were always on the lookout for trouble.

BAD BOY GEORGE BEST GETS A RED DISC

Southampton 4-1 Fulham
2 October 1976

George Best made his Fulham debut on 4 September 1976 and, typically, was an instant sensation with a goal after seventy-one seconds. The Fulham team of this period contained two world-class performers in George Best and Bobby Moore, plus the occasionally brilliant Rodney Marsh. They were exciting times at Craven Cottage and manager Alec Stock was confident that he had assembled a team who would push for promotion. Fulham's 2 October encounter against Southampton at The Dell was expected to provide an afternoon of football at its best, with Best, Moore and Marsh of Fulham and Mick Channon and Peter Osgood of the Saints all on view.

The 'ground full' signs were posted well before the kick-off. Southampton took the early initiative when MacDougall scored after just two minutes. Best and Marsh were expected to thrill the crowd with their silky skills, but it was the former Chelsea star Peter Osgood who stole the show. Now plying his trade for Southampton, Osgood showed all his old guile and skill to keep the home team in control of the game.

Southampton were leading 1-0 when George Best lost his cool. With sixty-seven minutes on the clock when Southampton were awarded a free-kick, the referee, L. Shapter, judged that Bobby Moore had fouled Stokes. As the Fulham players surrounded the referee to protest at his decision, Mick Channon quickly took the free-kick and Blyth headed the ball home. Best now went ballistic and was sent off for using 'foul and abusive language' against the referee. Best refused to go and his Fulham teammates continued to berate the official. George Best finally left the field of play when Fulham coach Bobby Campbell came on and led the Irishman to the dressing-room.

George Best is sent off by referee Les Shapler during Fulham's 4-1 defeat to Southampton in 1976. Best's Fulham teammate Bobby Moore stands third from the left.

The referee signalled to the two teams and the crowd that George Best was being sent off by holding up a red disc. This system was being used for the first time on this day and had been introduced after referee Ken Aston thought of the idea while waiting at a set of traffic lights. Best was beaten to the honour of becoming the first player to be red-disced in the English League by Blackburn's David Wagstaffe. The red and yellow discs were later replaced by cards, but were then withdrawn in 1981. They were reintroduced in 1987.

Southampton went on to beat Fulham 4-1, but George Best's sending-off was the main talking point that Saturday evening. Fulham boss Alec Stock told the press:

> It is like throwing the Christians to the lions. I'm absolutely certain that Best is singled out just because he is George Best. I don't condone bad language, but there is a worse evil – physical violence. There was plenty of that from Southampton. We are very much on George's side and I can safely say that Fulham will not be taking any disciplinary action against him.

George Best's fifth sending-off of his career did however result in another FA suspension.

ANDY GRAY'S KNOCKOUT PUNCH

Czechoslovakia 2–0 Scotland
World Cup qualifier
13 October 1976

Czechoslovakia were the reigning European Champions and were defending an unbeaten run that stretched to 23 games. Scotland clearly had their work cut out to get anything out of this World Cup qualifier. However, they could boast the likes of Gemmill, Dalglish, Buchan and Jordan in their line-up.

Bruce Rioch went close to giving Scotland the lead with a couple of rasping drives. Scotland were determined not to be overawed by the home team and their tackling was fierce. Gordon McQueen hit Goegh with a heavy tackle and the Czech defender was forced to limp out of the action. There then followed a spate of bookings, with McQueen, Gemmill, Buchan and Jorkemik all having their names taken for reckless challenges.

Aston Villa's young striker Andy Gray was making his fourth appearance for Scotland and it was turning out to be a severe test of his temperament. Gray was brave and feared no defender, but the Czech marking him on this occasion was giving him his sternest test to date. Right from the kick-off the young Scot was subjected to brutal and harsh treatment from Anton Ondrus, the home team's centre-half. Gray had been warned by Scotland manager Willie Ormond before the game to expect all the tricks of the trade from the Czechoslovakian players, who were masters at winding up the opposition.

With the tackling becoming fiercer by the minute, it was inevitable that the game was about to ignite and, as expected, the fists began to fly. With the half-time interval just minutes away, Andy Gray's tormentor, Ondrus, decided to elbow the Scotland striker in the face when the ball was nowhere near them. Gray was then pushed to the floor, which was the signal for the Scot to explode. He chased after the fleeing Ondrus, grabbed hold of him and hit him with a right hook. The Czech defender hit the deck and then began to roll around in agony, hoping that the official had not witnessed his sly elbow on Andy Gray. The referee was having none of it and when Ondrus got back to his feet he sent both of them off.

In the second half, the home team began to produce the outstanding football that they were capable of and two quick goals gave them a comfortable victory. Speaking about the incident in later years, Andy Gray knew that he had been conned. He said, 'Like a fool I had fallen for their trick and retaliated. It was one of the few moments when I lost my head on a football field. Perhaps it was the Glasgow boy inside me that had risen to the trouble.'

SENSATION AT THE VALLEY

Charlton Athletic 1–1 Maidstone
FA Cup third round
8 January 1979

The third round of the FA Cup generally provides something sensational. On this cold January day in 1979, First Division West Ham United were dumped out of the competition by Fourth Division minnows Newport County. Away from football, Geoff Boycott was providing sporting headlines in the world of cricket for allegedly telling an Australian MP to 'eff off'. According to reports, Liberal MP Jack Birney had sent Boycott a telegram prior to the fourth test stating that the Yorkshire batsman had, 'done to cricket what the Boston Strangler had done to door-to-door salesmen'. When Birney poked his nose into the England dressing room to commiserate with

Boycott for being out first ball, the Yorkshireman is alleged to have told him in no uncertain terms where to get off.

While the headlines should have belonged to woeful West Ham and the 'Boycott Affair' in Australia, it was at The Valley that the real sensation was taking place. Second Division Charlton were taking on Southern League Maidstone in the type of FA Cup third-round clash that football romantics love. Could the non-League outfit put one of the competition's previous winners out of the tournament? But it was not Maidstone's well deserved draw that had reporters clamouring to The Valley to get the low-down on one of football's greatest sensations in years, it was the fact that Charlton's star strikers, Derek Hales and Mike Flanagan, had been sent off for fighting with each other! Punch-ups between teammates have gone on since the game began, but have usually been confined to the training ground or, in the good old days, in the pub after the game had finished. This was the first time in English football history that members of a team had been dismissed for fighting amongst themselves.

The late 1970s had actually seen a spate of flare-ups between team-mates. In January 1977 Manchester United captain Martin Buchan was reported to have given his Old Trafford teammate Gordon Hill a clip round the ear when the United winger was reluctant to take up defensive duties. The match was against Coventry, which United won 2-0. A year later, in January 1978, Leeds pair Gordon McQueen and goalkeeper David Harvey were seen to exchange punches in an FA Cup third-round tie against Manchester City. After the game Leeds fined McQueen, who immediately asked for a transfer. He left to join Manchester United soon after the incident. In 1979 there were also scuffles between Northern Ireland teammates Gerry Armstrong and Terry Cochrane, in a game against England. Later on in the year the startled crowd at Old Trafford witnessed a punch-up between Brighton defender Gary Williams and his own goalkeeper Eric Steele. Both were booked by the referee after a stern lecture.

The reason for the Hales–Flanagan fisticuffs at The Valley was quite simple. Flanagan had apparently given Derek Hales a bollocking for being caught offside. Within seconds they were at each other's throats with a flurry of punches thrown. The referee sent them both for an early bath. All of this happened after Flanagan had equalised for Charlton after Maidstone had taken a surprise lead. Charlton held on for a draw, but by now the football was secondary. After the game Mick Flanagan was fined £250 by Charlton and Derek Hales had his contract terminated. A few days later however, Charlton had a change of heart and reinstated Hales at The Valley. He remained at the club until signing for Gillingham in 1984.

SCHUMACHER'S BRUTAL CHALLENGE ON BATTISTON

West Germany 3–3 France
World–Cup semi-final
8 July 1982
Germany won 5–4 on penalties

Toni Schumacher was a fine goalkeeper for West Germany during the 1980s, but he will always be remembered for his brutal challenge on Battiston of France during the 1982 World Cup semi-final. He might have got away with it at the time, but the image of Battiston lying unconscious on the ground after being knocked out by the German goalkeeper still remains in the memory of the millions who witnessed it on television.

Apart from Schumacher's challenge, the game itself was one of the finest in the history of the World Cup. The brilliant French aristocrats against the might of Germany was a match made in heaven. France could boast the silky skills of Platini, Giresse, Tigana and Rocheteau. Germany had the steel of Stielike, Kaltz and Reitner in their ranks.

The scene was set for a great game, with most neutrals watching around the world hoping for a French victory. As expected, Platini,

Giresse and Tigana of France weaved a pattern of footballing magic in midfield from the start, but hitting them on the break, Littbarski latched onto a blocked shot to put Germany ahead after only seventeen minutes. The French kept their composure and ten minutes later drew level from a Platini penalty. The scores remained level for the rest of the ninety minutes, but the real drama occurred when Battiston, who had replaced Genghini in the second half, raced through the German defence with only Schumacher standing between him and a certain France goal. The German goalkeeper raced from his penalty area and, using a combination of his knee and his thigh, knocked Battiston unconscious with a devastating blow to the Frenchman's head. As Battiston lay on the Seville turf gasping for breath it looked a certainty that Schumacher would receive a red card.

The spectators in the stadium and the millions watching on their televisions could see that the French player had been taken out by one of the most blatant professional fouls of all time. As Battiston was carried off to receive oxygen in the dressing-room, Schumacher awaited his fate. Then, unbelievably, Dutch referee C. Corver decided that Schumacher's assault on Battiston was an accidental collision and restarted the game without any action being taken against the German goalkeeper. His decision was regarded as one of the great scandals of World Cup history.

After an exciting period of extra time, which saw France build up a 3-1 lead only for Germany to draw level in the final minutes, the Germans won the game 5-4 on penalties. Germany may have been a fine side but the general consensus after the game was that they had cheated their way to the final. Fortunately (in the eyes of most neutral spectators), Italy stopped them taking the 1982 World Cup with an emphatic 3-1 victory in the final.

The German goalkeeper Toni Schumacher may have got off lightly for his brutal challenge on Battiston during the game, but it was an incident that he found hard to shake off throughout the rest of his career. In his autobiography he remarked:

West Germany goalkeeper Toni Schumacher commits probably the most brutal challenge in World Cup history as he collides with France's Battiston during the 1982 semi-final. Battiston had to be carried off unconscious. Schumacher went unpunished by the referee.

Since the 'foul' that I committed on Battiston in Spain in 1982, I'm perfectly aware that people have a negative view of me. For years I have been classified as some kind of wild animal and given a place in humanity's chamber of horrors. Because I was German, people thought I was made of the same metal as the torturers at Auschwitz. A guy with no human feelings whatsoever, and only one concern: not to let in any goals!

STRACHAN GETS WHACKED

Scotland 0–0 Uruguay
World Cup
13 June 1986

Scotland needed to beat Uruguay in this 1986 group game to progress to the latter stages of the World Cup. A draw was good enough for the South Americans to progress and they made sure that nothing was going to deny them, using every dirty trick in the book, which consisted of spitting, hair pulling, elbows in the face when the officials weren't looking... the Uruguayans were masters of them all.

The mayhem started as early as the first minute when Batista was given a straight red card for a vicious tackle on Gordon Strachan. Strachan had obviously been targeted as Scotland's main danger man and the South Americans were determined to nullify him as early as possible. Joel Quiniou, the French referee, was in no mood to give the Uruguay players the benefit of the doubt and Batista was dispatched to the dressing-room almost before the game had started. The referee might as well have signed his own death warrant. The Uruguay team had it in for him for the remainder of the match. As the two sets of players trouped off for the half-time interval, the South Americans even began to threaten him. He was quickly ushered to safety.

The second half followed the same pattern as the first with Uruguay feigning injury and time-wasting at every opportunity. When they decided to play football they looked outstanding and the ten men of Uruguay easily contained Scotland's eleven. The simmering atmosphere of imminent violence was always present and Cabrera was booked for an ugly foul and Acevedo was lucky not to be red-carded for a violent challenge on Strachan.

With Scotland's desperation for a winner growing by the minute, their tempers also began to fray. Narey and Nichol both found themselves in the referee's notebook for violent tackles as they attempted to up the tempo of the game, which the Uruguayans had somehow managed to keep at a relatively slow pace. With the Scotland supporters and all the neutrals in the stadium booing and jeering every touch of the ball by a Uruguay player, a winning goal for the Scots looked on the cards. The Scotland manager, Alex Ferguson, sent on Charlie Nicholas and Paul Sturrock for the last twenty minutes, but the Uruguayans' masterly use of time-wasting tactics never allowed Scotland to gain any real forward momentum. The game ended as a 0-0 draw, which meant that Uruguay were through to the final stages and Scotland were out. The Uruguay team left the field to a chorus of catcalls and jeers.

Gordon Strachan, who was subjected to a large section of the Uruguayan brutality, said it was the roughest game that he had ever experienced. Strachan remarked:

> We were being spat on, punched, had our hair pulled and were the victims of forearm smashes across the face when the officials were not looking. We were being punched in the back when we waited for a throw in to be taken. You would see a shadow or sense that someone was coming up behind you and then – WHACK!

BLOODBATH AT BRAMALL LANE

Sheffield United 1-0 Portsmouth
13 December 1986

Four players were sent off in this fixture, the first time this had happened in a Football League game since Crewe *v.* Bradford PA in 1955 game. The trouble began in the first half when Mick Kennedy of Portsmouth hit United's Kevin Arnott with a hard tackle. This set the tone for a game that rapidly degenerated into a brawl. In all, referee Kelvin Morton ended up sending off two players from each side, as well as handing out numerous cautions. Portsmouth, who were lying in second place in the Second Division at the time, were determined to get something from the match. Portsmouth manager Alan Ball said after the game, 'I asked my players to compete, but this was unbelievable.'

First to be dismissed was Billy Gilbert of Portsmouth, quickly followed by his teammate Mick Tait and United's Peter Beagrie. Tait and Beagrie had already received cautions and when they became involved in a violent scuffle, both were dismissed. An incensed Beagrie claimed after the game that he had been the victim of a headbutt. He said, 'When the linesman drew the ref's attention, I was pleased because Tait had butted me. I didn't believe it when he sent both of us off.'

Kevin Dillon of Portsmouth joined his teammates in the dressing room, just before half-time for a second bookable offence. The action did quieten down in the second half and United, despite some desperate rearguard action from the Portsmouth team who packed their eight remaining players into their penalty area for most of the second period, took the points after an own goal from Paul Mariner. When the sensational proceedings were over, United boss Billy McEwan shook his head and declared, 'The first thing I told my players at lunchtime on Saturday was to stay out of trouble because I sensed it would be a physical match. I didn't quite expect this, though.' Portsmouth manager Alan Ball whisked his players away from Bramall Lane without giving much away. As he boarded the team coach he muttered to one reporter, 'There was certainly plenty of atmosphere today.'

Note: Portsmouth's Mick Kennedy, the man whose tackle on United's Arnott initiated the trouble, was the following season fined £5,000 by the FA for bringing the game into disrepute. He had claimed in a newspaper article that he was the hardest man in football and this brought the wrath of the FA down upon him.

THE VIOLENT GAME
THAT NEVER WAS

Port Vale 0–0 Northampton Town
Littlewoods Cup
17 August 1987

Unlike present-day football, a time when as Joe Royle pointedly remarked, 'you can get sent off for heavy breathing,' the 1980s was a decade when a game with four red cards in it would have to be something of a bloodbath. Yet this 1987 Littlewoods Cup tie on a warm evening in August appears to have been nothing of the sort.

Staffordshire's *Evening Sentinel* newspaper described this as a game that 'failed to produce the passion of a schoolyard kick-about, yet four players were dismissed.' Vale supporters found it all hard to take in, but referee Vic Callow was determined to stamp his authority on the match and instigated two double-sendings-off. The trouble began in the thirty-third minute when Vale winger Paul Smith and Northampton's Steve Senior clashed after Smith had clattered into the Town player. The referee had no hesitation in sending both of the players for an early bath. Neither had received a yellow card before their dismissal.

Two more players were red-carded in the second half when Port Vale's Walker went in hard on Phil Chard of the away team. Chard took exception to this tackle and decided to take a kick at Walker who was lying prostrate on the turf. Once again the referee didn't hesitate to show both players the red card and Walker and a limping Chard trooped disconsolately off to the dressing-room. It was now nine against nine, yet most who witnessed the game claim it was hardly the bruising encounter that the bare statistics of the game would have us think. This bizarre encounter ended in a 0-0 draw.

Port Vale boss John Rudge said after the game that the dismissal of his two players did seem slightly harsh. 'Paul Smith wouldn't hurt a fly,' said Rudge. 'In fact, I wish he would show more aggression in his play.'

NOT AGAIN! ANOTHER BRAWL

Rangers 2-2 Celtic
17 October 1987

In the lead-up to the game there had been much discussion in the sporting media in Scotland about the man who had set in motion a football revolution at Rangers. Graeme Souness was not frightened of signing Roman Catholics or bringing English players to the club in his desire to make Rangers totally dominant in Scottish football.

Nor was Souness averse to signing players who, like himself, were not afraid to put themselves about when the occasion demanded it. This had led to a poor disciplinary record for himself and his team and he had even found himself confined to the stands following a suspension imposed on him after the last Old Firm encounter when he was found guilty of swearing at the referee outside the ground. This was after being sent off during the game.

With all of these factors in mind, the Scottish Football Association had warned Rangers that their future conduct was to be closely monitored. This 1987 game, however, was to leave the SFA scratching their heads in total disbelief. The outcome of this, one of the most violent Old Firm games in history, comprised court appearances for Rangers' Chris Woods, Terry Butcher and Graham Roberts, and Celtic's Frank McAvennie. The charge was disorderly conduct and breach of the peace on the field of play. Woods and Butcher were found guilty and fined. Roberts and McAvennie were acquitted. The Strathclyde police were of the opinion that violence on the field of play precipitated violence on the terraces and this was one of the main reasons that they decided to prosecute.

The game erupted in the sixteenth minute when McAvennie clashed with Rangers goalkeeper Woods. A free-for-all broke out and Roberts knocked McAvennie to the ground with his fists before order was restored. There were red cards for McAvennie and Woods and a booking for Terry Butcher, but Graham Roberts walked away

Celtic's Frank McAvennie receives a punch from Rangers goalkeeper Chris Woods during the 1987 Old Firm derby. Terry Butcher of Rangers looks on.

scot-free. Roberts then took over in the Rangers goal for the remainder of the game. Terry Butcher, who had already been booked in the first half, received his marching orders in the second period when he clattered into Celtic goalkeeper Allen McKnight. Despite late pressure from Celtic, Rangers held on for a 2-2 draw.

The *Daily Record* described the game as a catalogue of 'punching, kicking, elbowing, tripping and feigned injuries' and called immediately for a Scottish FA inquiry.

CHRISTMAS VIOLENCE AT GRIFFIN PARK

Brentford 2–2 Mansfield Town
19 December 1987

This festive-season encounter at Griffin Park exploded into a frenzy of violence in the eightieth minute. The outcome was two players from each side dismissed from the field of play. Until the punch-up late in the game, most reports state that although some of the tackling had been bordering on the reckless, in general it was not a particularly ill-tempered encounter.

All of this changed in the last ten minutes, however, when a free-for-all developed in the Mansfield Town penalty area. Referee Mike James moved in quickly to try and separate the warring factions before deciding who would be invited to take an early bath. First to be called over was Brentford's young defender Jamie Bates. After giving him a stern lecture, the referee showed him the red card. Colin Lee of Brentford was then next for the red-card treatment. Former Chelsea star Lee was not keen to leave the action, but he too then made his way to the dressing-rooms. By this time the Brentford faithful were clearly becoming agitated, thinking that only the home players were going to be sent off. The balance was restored, however, when Mansfield's veteran central defender George Foster and goalkeeper Kevin Hitchcock were also summoned to the referee who pointed them in the direction of the tunnel with a wave of his hand.

The crowd were stunned. Who could have anticipated that during the so-called season of goodwill to all men they would witness four players being sent off for only the third time in Football League history. The game was played out with Mansfield's Keith Cassells taking over in goal. Cassells was beaten by Gary Blisset for a Brentford equaliser, but then made a number of outstanding saves to earn Mansfield a point in a 2-2 draw.

PAUL 'JAWBREAKER' DAVIS

Arsenal 2-2 Southampton
17 September 1988

With the season barely a month old, there had already been some notable punch-ups, with Wimbledon's Vinny Jones staking his claim early on for the 'Punch of the Season' award. Jones was sent off in a pre-season friendly on the Isle of Wight for laying out a Shanklin defender. Jones' misdemeanour cost him a place in the Charity Shield game against Liverpool but even this effort was put in the shade by Paul Davis' humdinger of a punch that left Southampton's Glenn Cockerill nursing a broken jaw. *The Times*' correspondent described the blow as 'a vicious left hook'. Davis' display of punching power certainly hit the headlines back in September 1988, particularly as the ITV cameras just happened to be at Highbury to capture it for posterity.

The game itself was a bad-tempered affair right from the kick-off. Arsenal boss George Graham claimed that Southampton were time-wasting from the start. The fact that the referee added on nearly ten minutes' stoppage time at the end of play gave some credence to Graham's claims. With the tackles flying in, Arsenal's Nigel Winterburn found himself in the referee's notebook for a brutal challenge on one of the Southampton players. The main violent act of the game, however, was not witnessed by the match officials. With the play up at the other end of the pitch, Paul Davis took exception to something Glenn Cockerill said or did by laying him out cold with a punch that Mike Tyson would have been proud of. None of the officials witnessed it, but the Arsenal bench decided to act promptly and pulled Davis out of the action. With Cockerill receiving treatment, Richardson came on for Davis. Cockerill played on, nursing a sore jaw that was later found out to be broken.

The match ended in a 2-2 draw, but the repercussions went on for weeks. Southampton boss Chris Nicholl said after the game that four of his players came away from the match with injuries and that he felt cheated. Southampton's main danger man, Matt Le Tissier, came in for some harsh treatment and limped off injured during the game, but the main talking point was Davis' punch on Cockerill. What had driven the Arsenal midfielder to act in this way remains a mystery to this day. The FA, after viewing ITV footage of the incident, fined Davis £3,000 and banned him for nine matches. Cockerill himself decided not to take the matter any further. Arsenal were furious that ITV had allowed the disciplinary hearing to view footage of Davis punching Cockerill and banned their cameras from Highbury.

PRE-BONFIRE NIGHT FIREWORKS AT HIGHBURY

Arsenal 4-3 Norwich City
4 November 1989

This bruising encounter between Arsenal and Norwich, who were both riding high near the top of the First Division, ended in a mass brawl and an FA inquiry. The outcome of the inquiry was a £50,000 fine for Norwich and a £20,000 fine for Arsenal. Until the final minutes of the match both teams had put on a superb exhibition of attacking football. Norwich led 2-0 at the interval, but Arsenal fought back and, with just seconds remaining, the score stood at 3-3.

Referee George Tyson then awarded Arsenal a penalty and Lee Dixon stepped up to give the home team an unexpected 4-3 victory. It was when a jubilant Alan Smith attempted to collect the ball from the back of the Norwich net that the fun started. Smith was punched by a Norwich player and sustained a gash over his eye. Within seconds it became a free-for-all with arguments raging and punches being thrown in a frenzy of violence. The referee decided to take no action. To be honest, he didn't really know where to start, with most of the players on the field taking some part in the brawl.

It took the match officials and astonished London police to bring the fighting to an end. With a semblance of order restored, the final whistle came as a blessing for all concerned, but even as the two teams left the pitch, bitter arguments and recriminations were still raging. Norwich's Andy Townsend, who was not even playing in the game, decided to have a go at his Eire teammate David O'Leary. Arsenal boss George Graham then turned on Townsend and gave him a stern ear-bashing. In the aftermath of the Highbury brawl, which was witnessed that evening by *Match of the Day* viewers, the sports press were unanimous in their condemnation of the two teams. Clive White of *The Times* wrote, 'Fighting among players on this scale and ferocity cannot be overlooked, particularly when it requires the intervention of the police to bring order.'

A TALE OF
NATIONALISTIC HATRED

Dynamo Zagreb 0–0 Red Star Belgrade
13 May 1990
(Match abandoned)

The Red Star Belgrade team of the early 1990s was outstanding and won the European Cup in 1991. Soon after their European triumph, the Red Star team disintegrated as Yugoslavia became embroiled in a bloody civil war. Throughout the 1980s, conflict between the Serbia and Croatia regions had been simmering and it frequently manifested itself during games between the Serbian Red Star Belgrade and the Croatian Dynamo Zagreb.

On 13 May 1990 Yugoslavian First Division Champions Red Star travelled from Belgrade for an end–of–season fixture against Dynamo Zagreb. Nothing was at stake points–wise, with Red Star having won the title some weeks earlier. The match took place at the Maksimir Stadium in Zagreb and thousands of Red Star supporters travelled from Belgrade to cheer on their team.

The authorities in Zagreb were expecting trouble after the Croatian Democratic Union had defeated the Communists in recent elections. Red Star and their followers were extremely nationalistic and there were suspicions that the match would be used to whip up support for the Serbs' aims of stopping the Yugoslav federation being torn apart. Croatia, like most of the other Yugoslav republics, had ambitions of becoming an independent state. With the threat of civil war in the air the Dynamo Zagreb encounter against Red Star Belgrade in May 1990 looked a certainty to become a violent confrontation.

The fighting began on the terraces before the match had actually kicked off. The mainly Serb police force used batons and tear gas to restore order to the ground. Incredibly, the authorities allowed the game to take place. During the first period of play the fighting on the terraces flared up again and this time it spread onto the pitch. The police once again fought to restore order, but there were accusations after the game that they mainly seemed to be attacking the Dynamo fans. Two of the Dynamo team began to fight with the police, one of them being future AC Milan star Zvonimir Boban. Boban was seen to kick one of the policemen in the head as he fought to stop them attacking the Dynamo fans. Boban was later charged with assault by the police, but the court's decision was that he was merely defending himself and the young spectators surrounding him. His actions made him a national hero in Croatia, but he quickly had to flee the country when hostilities throughout the region really took a turn for the worse. Boban was also dropped from the Yugoslavia team that competed in the 1990 World Cup.

After the riot had died down, over seventy fans needed hospital treatment for their injuries. Dynamo's manager said after the game that 'the trouble could have been prevented, but the police failed to take adequate security precautions.' He also said that the police were too lenient with the followers of Red Star, but dealt with the home crowd very severely. 'It was a miracle that no one was killed,' remarked one of the spectators leaving the ground. Sadly, within a few years, many who attended the 1990 Dynamo Zagreb against Red Star Belgrade fixture would lose their lives in the conflict that swept through the region soon after.

MARADONA GETS A KICKING

Argentina 0–1 Cameroon
World Cup
8 June 1990

Cameroon provided the shock of the 1990 World Cup by beating reigning champions Argentina in the opening game. Cameroon knew that they had little chance of matching Maradona and his teammates when it came to football expertise, so drastic measures were the order of the day.

Maradona was clattered as early as the ninth minute when Massing was booked for a brutal tackle from behind. Massing was under strict orders from Cameroon's Russian manager, Valery Nepomniachy, to man-mark the brilliant Maradona throughout the game. Ndip, the Cameroon defender, gave Massing a break from his man-marking activities when he hit Maradona later. The tackle was in fact so high that Maradona was left bleeding from stud marks to his shoulder. The lenient referee only booked Ndip for this misdemeanour. Sensini of Cameroon was then booked for deliberate handball.

Although Argentina found themselves on the receiving end of some violent challenges, the 73,000 Milan crowd cheered every reckless tackle, particularly when Maradona was the victim of the rough stuff. At this stage in his career Maradona was the star performer for Napoli, who had just taken the Italian title from AC Milan. In the second half, referee M. Vautrot's patience snapped when he sent off Kana for a professional foul on Caniggia.

Unbelievably Cameroon then took the lead when the Argentina goalkeeper Pupido inexplicably allowed a weak header from Omann to slip through his hands for a sloppy goal. The crowd went berserk

Diego Maradona is left clutching his shoulder after Ndip of Cameroon leaves his calling card. The tackle was in fact so high that the great Argentinian was left bleeding from stud marks to his upper body. Cameroon's 1-0 victory over Argentina during the 1990 World Cup was one of the greatest upsets in the tournament's history.

and whistled every attempt by a lacklustre Argentina team to draw level. Every time Maradona received the ball he was greeted with catcalls and booing from the San Siro spectators. There was some slight relief for Maradona near the end when his shadow, Massing, was sent off near the end for a second bookable offence. Although Cameroon ended the match with just nine men, they held on for a victory that shocked the world of football. Although Maradona had had to endure some violent tackles, he refused to condemn the tactics of the Cameroon team at the end of the game. 'What's past is past. Cameroon won because they were better than us,' remarked the Argentinian superstar.

RIJKAARD'S INFAMOUS
VOLLEY AT VOLLER

West Germany 2-1 Holland
World Cup
24 June 1990

This 1990 World Cup second-round encounter provided the most notorious volley of spit ever seen on a football field. Spitting in full view of the television cameras is nothing new. Older followers of the game can still recall watching *Match of the Day* in May 1967, when Manchester United star Pat Crerand was caught on camera spitting at the Stoke half-back Tony Allen.

Over the years there have been other occasions when spitting has hit the headlines, such as Arsenal's Patrick Vieira spitting in the face of West Ham's Neil Ruddock during a heated London derby in October 1999. In recent years Bolton's El-Hadji Diouf has also proved himself quite adept at using a mouthful of phlegm against the opposition, but you would have to go a long way to surpass Frank Rijkaard's spitting display against Rudi Voller of Germany during the 1990 World Cup.

The Holland against West Germany clash was probably the greatest game of the 1990 tournament. The two nations care little for each other when it comes to football and extra tension was added to the game by the fact that Holland had three AC Milan players in their ranks and the Germans three Inter Milan stars.

The game was a physical encounter from the start and it provided fabulous entertainment for the millions watching on television. The football on display may have been hard, but it was also brilliant. The Dutch, with the likes of Gullit and van Basten in their ranks, looked the most likely to take control of the game early on, but spurned some great goalscoring opportunities. In a match played at a high tempo, the tackles were meaty right from the start and Holland's van Tiggelen was lucky not to find himself in trouble after a brutal tackle on Littbarski after just thirty seconds.

The game had threatened to explode right from the kick-off and midway through the first half Rijkaard brought down Voller with a heavy tackle. It was Voller who found himself in the referee's note-book for dissent after arguing about the severity of the Dutchman's challenge. Voller then made contact with the Holland goalkeeper van Breukelen when challenging for the ball and Rijkaard came to the aid of his keeper. Voller and Rijkaard then became embroiled in a flurry of pushing and shoving and the referee, J. Loustau, had seen enough. The Argentinian official showed them both the red card, but the slanging match carried on as they walked to the dressing rooms. Rijkaard was then seen to lean over and release a volley of spit into Voller's hair as they walked from the pitch. The German striker could not believe it; neither could the millions watching on television. As the German wiped the spit from his blonde locks, officials kept the two players apart until they reached the dressing-room area.

After the sendings-off the game settled down and both teams put on a great display of European football at it's finest. Klinsmann put Germany ahead early in the second half and Brehme added a second. Five minutes from the end, a Koeman penalty gave the Dutch hope, but Germany held on for a famous victory. Although the game was a fine spectacle, all the talk at the end was of the sending-off incident. Rijkaard was an outstanding performer for club and country throughout his career, but the spitting incident did tarnish his image somewhat.

KICKING AND BORING

Argentina 0-1 West Germany
World Cup final
8 July 1990

The final of the 1990 World Cup, held in the Stadio Olimpico, Rome, was a tedious, sterile affair. Argentina's outstanding victorious teams of the 1978 and 1986 World Cup finals were a fading memory. Whether the 1990 team could play football we never found out. They basically sulked their way through to the final, doing as little as

Referee Keith Hackett attempts to break up a punch-up between Arsenal and Manchester United during a fiery 1990 encounter at Old Trafford.

possible in the way of football to get there. Even the great Maradona appeared a shadow of the magnificent footballer who set the 1986 tournament alight with his genius.

Germany were as organised and single-minded as ever in pursuit of victory. Any football that was played came in the main from the Germans. Argentina appeared to be playing with a penalty shoot-out in mind and ventured into the German half only on rare occasions. The game sprang to life in the sixty-eighth minute when Klinsmann reacted to an over-zealous tackle from Monzon. Monzon and the rest of his Argentinian teammates could not believe it when the referee showed him the red card. Monzon now had the dubious distinction of becoming the first player to be sent off in a World Cup final.

Germany seized the initiative and Brehme gave them the lead from the penalty spot six minutes from time. Argentina, by now clearly in an agitated frame of mind, had another player dismissed three minutes from the final whistle when Dezotti was red-carded for forcefully attempting to get the ball off a time-wasting Kohler. In the ensuing melee that followed, Maradona also had his name taken for dissent. The most tedious World Cup final of all time is now remembered mainly because of the double sending-off, nothing else.

THE BATTLE OF OLD TRAFFORD

Manchester United 0–1 Arsenal
20 October 1990

Less than one year earlier, Arsenal had been up before the FA for their part in the all-out brawl that took place in their 1989 game against Norwich. On that occasion they were fined £20,000. Now Arsenal once again found themselves facing disciplinary action by the FA after twenty-one of the players on view became involved in a mass dust-up. The trouble had been simmering for some time before Anders Limpar of Arsenal went in hard on United's Denis

Irwin. Within seconds Nigel Winterburn became involved and the only player who stayed out of the mass tugging and jostling spectacle on view was the Arsenal goalkeeper David Seaman.

Before this particular flare-up, Paul Ince of United had deposited Limpar on to the sidelines, and McClair and Winterburn had also come close to blows. But it was the Limpar tackle on Irwin that led to the major blow-up of the game, a fact reinforced by United boss Alex Ferguson. Ferguson recalled, 'The explosion came when Limpar went into a tackle with Irwin. He could have seriously hurt him. It carried on from there and for a couple of minutes everyone piled in.' Arsenal took the points with a 1-0 victory but an FA inquiry was inevitable.

The FA disciplinary committee were quick to act after the game and decided to fine both clubs £50,000 and dock Arsenal two points and United one point. The FA decision infuriated United boss Ferguson, who stated, 'I went to the hearing and I got the distinct impression that one or two there didn't care for Manchester United. The meeting was a shambles.'

Arsenal manager George Graham denied that most of the two sets of players were involved in the brawl. 'At least ten of them were trying to stop rather than start trouble,' said Graham. The club itself decided to fine just five of their team for their part in the fight: Paul Davis, David Rocastle, Anders Limpar, Michael Thomas and Nigel Winterburn all had two weeks' wages taken off them. 'It was one occasion when the "all-for-one-and-one-for-all" team spirit that I have worked so hard to generate at Arsenal boiled over,' reflected Graham.

ERIC'S RUMBLE IN TURKEY

Galatasaray 0–0 Manchester United
European Cup
3 November 1993

Manchester United were dumped out of Europe after failing to beat Turkish champions Galatasaray in a tense, heated encounter. The atmosphere generated by the Istanbul club's fanatical followers has often been described as the most hostile in Europe – though Alex Ferguson made light of this, saying, 'If you've been to a wedding in Glasgow, you certainly wouldn't be bothered about going to Galatasaray' – and on this particular occasion the Galatasaray fans exceeded themselves. Over 40,000 passionate Turks, some waving banners that read 'Welcome to Hell', were baying for United's blood. United were even met at the airport by large groups of Galatasaray followers jeering their every move.

The game itself was not particularly violent; that is, until Eric Cantona decided to put himself about. With United desperate for a victory, and the home team content with a draw, Cantona thought that the Galatasaray goalkeeper was time-wasting by holding onto the ball for too long and jumped onto the track surrounding the pitch to retrieve it himself. There was also a Galatasaray player down injured at the time but Eric decided he was just play-acting. The goalkeeper would not let go of the ball so Cantona decided to kick it out of his hands, also elbowing the keeper in the ribs for good measure. The Turkish players surrounded the United forward, looking for revenge, but the referee intervened and all was calm again.

At the final whistle all hell broke loose when Cantona decided to approach the referee to give him some tips on his refereeing technique. This time, with the game ended, the red card was shown to Cantona. A scuffle then flared up in the tunnel and police attacked Cantona and United captain Bryan Robson. Cantona was left with a sore head and Robson needed stitches in a wound to his hand. An outraged Cantona told the press after the game, 'It was scandalous.

Eric Cantona clashes with Galatasary players during Manchester United's 1993 game against the Turkish Champions. Cantona received a red card.

I was attacked by a policeman. The red card doesn't bother me. All I did was tell him he was a bad referee.'

MAYHEM AT THE PALACE

Crystal Palace 1-1 Manchester United
25 January 1995

This was the day when 'the shit hit the fan', were the type of barbed joke doing the rounds after Manchester United's idiosyncratic but outstanding footballing talent Eric Cantona launched an astonishing attack on a Crystal Palace fan who had hurled racist abuse at the French star. The outcome of it all for Cantona was a £20,000 fine by Manchester United, a £10,000 fine by the FA, an eight-month ban from football and 120 hours of community service.

The flashpoint came in the second half when Cantona received his marching orders for kicking Palace defender Richard Shaw. On his way to the dressing-room Cantona decided to teach the taunting Palace fan a lesson and ran into the crowd and scissor-kicked him before launching a couple of blows with his fists at his chosen target. Spectators in the vicinity of the Cantona attack stood open-mouthed with astonishment. The football was now of secondary importance; this was sensational behaviour by anyone's standards. It had happened before, however, when the legendary Everton striker William Ralph 'Dixie' Dean was confronted on the pitch in a menacing manner by a Spurs' supporter (he called Dean a 'black bastard') after a 1930s First Division encounter in London. Dean, thinking the fan was about to attack him, decided to take no chances and laid the man out flat with a right uppercut. That confrontation hardly caused a murmur in the press. Cantona's indiscretion was headline news for weeks.

Paul Ince also became involved in the fracas that followed and it took police, stewards, and Cantona's teammate Peter Schmeichel to help restore order. The red card that Cantona had received was his fifth in the previous thirteen months. Asked about the Selhurst Park incident recently, Cantona shrugged his shoulders and said, 'That night is confined to the dustbin of history. I prefer to remember the sweeter moments.' For his part in the Crystal Palace debacle, Paul Ince was charged with common assault by police for attacking a Palace supporter. The case went to court, but Ince was found not guilty.

BIG DUNC IN TROUBLE AGAIN

Leicester City 2–2 Everton
4 March 1995

A stormy clash at Filbert Street ended with nine-man Everton holding out for a draw when a win looked a certainty. Everton were coasting to an easy victory after building up a two-goal lead in the first half. After the break, with Leicester as desperate as the Merseysiders for points to help them pull away from the relegation zone, the game took a violent turn for the worse. Vinny Samways had a kick at Mike Galloway after the two had clashed with the ball up the other end of the pitch. Referee Paul Durkin sent the Everton midfielder off.

This incident certainly brought the game to the boil and it was Duncan Ferguson who was next to go for an alleged elbow on Leicester's Jimmy Willis. Ferguson, who had been involved in a heated verbal battle with fellow Scot Mike Galloway throughout the game, clearly lost his cool and had to pay the price.

Furious Everton boss Joe Royle said after the game, 'I can't explain how angry I am. It was an absolute disgrace. Samways was done for retaliation and god knows what Duncan Ferguson was thinking about. There were two brainstorms out there. I'll be taking action against the two of them!'

Leicester manager Mark McGhee, who was delighted that his team had fought back to earn a point, told the press that Ferguson's red card was harsh: 'Fergie suffers from his reputation and it didn't look to me like there was any intent when he caught my player with his elbow,' said McGhee.

THE BATTLE OF ANCONA

Ancona 1-2 Birmingham City
Anglo-Italian Cup
15 November 1995

This was an ill-tempered encounter that saw two players from each side booked and two Ancona players stretchered off in the first half. Throughout the game one scuffle followed another and incredibly, at one stage, the Birmingham physiotherapist was attacked by an Ancona player while flying to treat Paul Tait for a head injury.

During another incident, the Ancona trainer, Massimo Cacciatori ran on to the pitch and grabbed Birmingham's Ricky Otto by the throat after Birmingham were awarded a free-kick. Other Birmingham players that Cacciatori was alleged to have assaulted were Paul Tait and Joe Martin, who was sitting in the dugout at the time.

The violence didn't stop at the conclusion of play. If anything, it got worse. Players and officials of both sides decided to carry on the brutality after the final whistle and a mass brawl broke out. In the melee, it was alleged that Cacciatori was pushed to the floor and kicked in the face by Birmingham players. The outcome of the dressing-room brawl left match referee John Lloyd of Wrexham needing hospital treatment for a broken hand and Ancona's trainer Cacciatori with a fractured cheek and a cut eye. Lloyd had broken his hand after he fell trying to break up the brawl. Birmingham manager Barry Fry accused Cacciatori of assaulting three of his players and added, 'If I did what he did, I'd expect to be kicked out of football.' Ancona club president Francoesco Contadini said, 'This was one of the most violent games ever seen in Italy. It was deplorable to witness what happened in that passageway and to see our trainer covered in blood.'

Birmingham's Paul Tait, recalling the game, said:

I went in for a tackle and the next thing I knew they were coming at me from all angles. I saw a fat guy running towards me out of the corner of my eye – I thought it was Barry Fry at first – and he screamed, 'You're dead'. It was their coach. Then all hell broke loose. It was happening all over the pitch. I don't think I have ever played in a match like that before.

MOSCOW MAYHEM

Spartak Moscow 3-0 Blackburn Rovers
European Cup
23 November 1995

Blackburn's first tilt at the European Cup ended in complete disarray. Kenny Dalglish's boys had won the League title for the first time in eighty-one years and were quietly fancied to do well in the Champions League. When Blackburn ran out to face Spartak Moscow at a freezing cold Luzhniki Stadium in November 1995, they knew that a victory was needed to give them a chance of reaching the quarter-finals. Dalglish had said before the game that his team would fight all the way. What he didn't expect was to witness them fighting each other.

With just five minutes played, Graeme Le Saux and David Batty both went for a pass from Newell. The two players collided and then became involved in a furious exchange of words near the touchline. Punches were then exchanged and only the rapid intervention of the Blackburn captain, Tim Sherwood, averted a full-scale bout of fisticuffs. The Moscow crowd could not believe their eyes and Blackburn were fortunate that the referee decided to ignore the incident and carry on with the game.

After the Le Saux–Batty flare-up, Blackburn actually had their best spell of the game and put the Spartak goal under some pressure. Then, just when the away team were beginning to take control, there was another heated exchange of views between several Blackburn players. This time the incident involved Hendry and Sherwood after the Blackburn skipper had lost the ball. Once again their Rovers teammates had to move in quickly to stop the argument erupting into something more serious.

After this flare-up, Spartak took the lead and began to take control of the tie. With the English Champions now in total disarray, Spartak built up a three-goal lead in the second half. Blackburn and Colin Hendry's dismal night was completed fifteen minutes from

Tim Sherwood, the Blackburn Rovers captain, steps in to stop his teammates Graeme Le Saux and David Batty fighting during his side's infamous European Cup game against Spartak Moscow. The referee ignored their sensational punch-up and carried on with the game.

the end when Hendry received a red card. The Blackburn defender was adjudged to have fouled Tikhonov when the Spartak attacker was clear through on goal.

After the game an apologetic Graeme Le Saux, his punching hand swathed in a bandage, told the press, 'There are reasons why I hit Batty, but I admit that my behaviour was very unprofessional.' Spartak boss, Oleg Romantseuer, said he was astounded by the Blackburn team's behaviour. He said, 'It's the first time I have seen players from the same team settling a score with a fist fight. Before the game I told my players that they would be up against a team ready to fight for each other for ninety minutes, but not against each other! After the fight I felt a team so split could be beaten very easily.'

The Le Saux–Batty punch-up was just one of a series of flare-ups between teammates during the 1990s. In September 1993, Liverpool goalkeeper Bruce Grobbelaar threw a punch at Steve McManaman during a game against Everton. McManaman fought back before they were separated. In August 1994 Hearts' captain Craig Levin and teammate Graeme Hogg became involved in a violent fracas during their team's pre-season friendly against Raith. Both were sent off and Hogg had to be dispatched to the dressing-room on a stretcher. The Scottish FA held an inquiry and banned both Levin and Hogg for ten games.

In March 1996 Colin Murphy, manager of Notts County, and Shaun Murphy, one of his players, became involved in a heated argument that resulted in a fracas in the tunnel after their game at Blackpool. The FA charged them both with misconduct.

In April 1996 Hartlepool player/manager Keith Houchen and his goalkeeper Brian Horne became embroiled in an on-pitch punch-up after their opponents Gillingham took the lead. After the game, Houchen told reporters that he intended fining Horne, 'Nobody grabs me by the throat,' he exclaimed.

The 1990s ended on yet another televised punch-up between teammates when Everton's Don Hutchison launched an attack on his Goodison teammate Richard Gough. Gough managed to keep his cool better than the clearly agitated Hutchison as their Everton colleagues battled to retain order. After the game Hutchison apologised to Gough and told the press that his behaviour was out of order. Everton boss Walter Smith said, 'It was just a clash. The players have sorted it out for themselves. These things happen in football. As far as I am concerned the matter is now finished.' Hutchison took Gough for a meal later that evening to patch things up. Clearly if you wanted to witness teammates at war on the pitch, the 1990s was certainly the golden period.

VINNY AND THE SQUEALING PIG

Chelsea 1-2 Wimbledon
26 December 1995

Vinny Jones would end this Boxing Day game with the eleventh sending-off of his stormy career. For a London derby, the first half had not been particularly physical – apart, that is, from a bone-crunching tackle on Petrescu by Jones that led to a yellow card. Jones, in fact, spent most of the first half dishing out menacing stares rather than hard tackles, but all of this was to change in the second period.

Vinny Jones had been seconded to stick like a leech for the duration of the game to the Chelsea manager and playmaker Ruud Gullit. Ten minutes into the second half, Jones carried out his instructions a little bit too literally when he crashed into Gullit from behind and his second bookable offence meant a red card was inevitable. Wimbledon held on with ten men to record a famous victory. 'I played the ball,' pleaded Jones at the after-match press conference, but nobody took much notice. The following morning everyone in the game took notice when an exclusive interview given by Vinny to a tabloid contained a whole string of non-complimentary remarks about Ruud Gullit and other foreign imports. 'My pot-bellied pig doesn't squeal as much as Gullit,' was a typical sentiment expressed in the article, and for this Jones would face an FA charge.

Wimbledon owner Sam Hammam was none too pleased with Vinny's antics and said, 'The foul on Gullit was wrong and this article is wrong. Vinny has let himself, the team and the club down. He must accept the consequences.'

FIASCO AT IBROX

Rangers 3-0 Hearts
14 September 1996

In one of the most amazing games that Scottish football had ever seen, four Hearts players received the red card. If one more Hearts player had been dismissed, the referee would have been forced to abandon the game. The only other occasion that four players from the same side had been sent off in a match was in the 1994 Airdrie *v.* Stranraer game. Stranraer ended up, like Hearts, with only seven players on the field.

Pasquale Bruno of Hearts was first to go. The tough Italian defender had built up a bad disciplinary record for himself in Serie A and appeared to be determined to display the physical side of his game to Scottish fans. After raking Laudrup with his studs in the first half, he was sent off for a second bookable offence. Bruno appeared to be totally unconcerned and smiled and raised his arms to the jeering Ibrox crowd as he left the field. David Weir was next to go after clashing with Gordon Durie. After an eyeball-to-eyeball confrontation with the Rangers player, Weir appeared to catch Durie with his forehead.

Just one minute later, Neil Pointon was also red-carded for using foul and abusive language at the assistant referee. Pointon had been booked in the first half for having a dig at McInnes of Rangers. The madness had still not ended. With three Hearts players now taking an early bath, Paul Ritchie was also found guilty of shouting something that was deemed unacceptable towards the assistant referee. At this stage, Hearts chairman Chris Robinson appeared to be keen to bring an end to his club's participation and seemed to beckon them to come off, but their seven remaining players stayed on the park. Rangers' captain Richard Gough appealed to referee Gerry Evans to show some leniency towards Hearts, probably aware that one more dismissal would bring the game to a halt, and Rangers' 3-0 lead would count for nothing. Hearts survived the remaining minutes

with no more sendings-off and Rangers ran out easy 3-0 winners.
The Hearts team stormed out of the ground after the game without
uttering a word to anyone. A Scottish Football Association inquiry
was immediately called for.

BARE-KNUCKLE FOOTBALL
AT SALTERGATE

Chesterfield 1-2 Plymouth Argyle
22 February 1997

1997 was the year that one of English football's lesser clubs, Chesterfield,
hit the headlines in a big way. Their fabulous FA Cup run had
football fans throughout the land totally engrossed. They reached
the semi-final stage of the competition, matching the achievement
of Plymouth Argyle, who had been the last Third Division club to
go so far in the cup, in 1984. Only some dodgy refereeing decisions
in their semi-final clash against Middlesbrough robbed them of the
chance to make FA Cup history by reaching the final.

Chesterfield did, however, take part in a match during the 1996/97
season that became a record breaker in its own right. By the end of
their home match against Plymouth in February 1997 five players
had been sent off. This set a new record for the most dismissals in a
Football League game. Wigan and Bristol Rovers did go on to equal
this dubious achievement later in the year when one Wigan and four
Rovers players were red-carded in a December 1997 encounter, but
Chesterfield and Plymouth did it first.

Chesterfield were defending a five-month unbeaten home record
and were looking good for a promotion spot at the end of the
season. Plymouth were desperate for points themselves in order not
to become embroiled in the relegation dogfight when the season
drew to a close. Mick Jones, the Plymouth boss, had told his team

that they were not to come away from Saltergate without at least a point. When the game started, Chesterfield, who should have been on a high after their sensational victory over Nottingham Forest in the FA Cup the previous week, looked like they were instead suffering from victory-celebration hangovers. Despite the fact that Argyle were reduced to ten men after Mauge was dismissed in the first half for a violent tackle, the West Country team went into a two-goal lead.

Chesterfield pressed forward in the second half in a desperate attempt to take something from the game. Urged on by their supporters, Howard gave Chesterfield a glimmer of hope five minutes from time when he reduced the deficit to one goal. Plymouth desperately hung on as Chesterfield pounded the Argyle defence with just minutes to play. Chesterfield won a corner and threw everyone into the Argyle penalty area in a desperate attempt to force an equaliser. When the corner was taken, shots were blocked in the packed penalty area before the ball seemed to nestle in a scrum of players. Bruce Grobbelaar, who was playing in goal for Plymouth, was knocked to the ground. This was the signal for a full-scale fracas, with the prostrate Grobbelaar one of the few members of the two teams not involved. Fists and boots were flying as coaching staff and Chesterfield stewards intervened in a desperate battle to stop the punch-up.

Eventually peace was restored and the referee did not know where to begin when it came to dishing out red cards. When the dust settled, Darren Carr, the tough-tackling Chesterfield defender, who at 6ft 2in and thirteen stone was not a man that Argyle should have messed about with, and another Chesterfield giant, 6ft 2in Kevin Davies, were the home players to get their marching orders. For Plymouth, James and Logan joined their teammate Ronnie Mauge in taking an early bath. A few supporters who had made their way onto the pitch during the fracas were ushered away by police. When the game ended, a groggy Bruce Grobbelaar, sporting a black eye, had to be helped off the pitch by the Argyle backroom staff.

In the aftermath of this extraordinary encounter, the police issued a statement saying that they were considering taking action over the violent scenes at Saltergate. Simon Wilde, reporting on the game for *The Times*, said, 'The disgraceful fracas that erupted two minutes before the finish would not have looked out of place in a Wild West saloon.' The Plymouth manager, Mick Jones, would only say, 'I may have wound up my players too much before the game, but I have to be careful what I say.'

The match referee, Richard Poulain, remarked, 'It was frightening. It was the worst brawl that I have ever seen and I never want to see it repeated. I've just come back from a holiday, now I'll need another one to get over this.'

DI CANIO BLOWS A FUSE

Celtic 0–1 Rangers
16 March 1997

This Old Firm encounter had the added spice of Celtic attempting to stop Rangers emulating their record nine consecutive championships. If Rangers came out of the game victorious they would be virtually assured of the title. As usual in Old Firm matches the action was fast and furious. The only goal of the game came in the forty-fourth minute when Celtic failed to clear Albertz's free-kick and, after Durrant crossed the ball back into the penalty area, Laudrup scored from close range.

Celtic huffed and puffed in the second half and Paulo Di Canio, who had hit the bar in the first half, gave everything for the cause, but in the main they rarely threatened Dibble in the Rangers goal. Tempers began to fray as Celtic pushed for an equaliser and the game deteriorated into a bad-tempered encounter. Red cards were inevitable and Mark Hately was first to go when the Rangers striker became involved in an altercation with Kerr, the Celtic goalkeeper. The striker appeared to butt him. Ten minutes later, Malky Mackay, the hard Celtic central defender, was also dismissed for a second bookable offence. He had brought down Laudrup with an illegal tackle.

When the final whistle went, Di Canio and Ian Ferguson, who had been goading each other all afternoon, became involved in a heated argument. Di Canio claimed that Ferguson swore at him and he decided to chase after the Rangers player to sort him out. Their teammates managed to keep the two of them apart, which was fortunate for Ferguson as Di Canio appeared to have lost all control.

After the game the Italian was adamant that Ferguson had a lucky escape. He said, 'It was obvious that he was terrified. I don't think I have ever been so angry in my life. There is no question in my mind that I would have beaten him to a pulp. I would have hurt him severely.'

FOWLER GETS A BLOODY NOSE

Everton 1-1 Liverpool
16 April 1997

Merseyside derbies are always passionate and this one was no different. Liverpool were desperate for the three points to help them keep in touch with Manchester United in the race for the Premiership title. Everton were fighting to avoid relegation. The scene was set and the tackles flew in thick and fast. Jamie Redknapp gave Liverpool a twenty-fifth-minute lead, but Duncan Ferguson levelled the score in the sixty-fourth minute.

Trouble had been brewing between Everton defender David Unsworth and Liverpool's Robbie Fowler for some time before it boiled over into a flurry of fists. Unsworth hit the Liverpool striker with a hard tackle from behind and the pair traded blows before teammates separated the warring duo. Fowler had blood pouring from a nosebleed and he decided to have another go at the Everton player, even after the referee had shown them both the red card.

Liverpool physio Mark Leather and coach Ronnie Moran jumped in to lead Fowler down the tunnel. Liverpool manager Roy Evans ran onto the pitch to argue the toss with referee Stephen Lodge, but his decision had been made and Evans' gesture was to prove futile.

Everton held on to gain the point that was needed to help them escape the threat of the drop, and the two points that Liverpool dropped meant that the title was now almost certainly Manchester United's. Alex Ferguson was to leave Goodison Park a happy man. Roy Evans, still unhappy about Fowler's dismissal, said, 'If the referee had blown when Unsworth went through the back of Robbie, the whole sending-off incident could have been avoided'.

THE MOST SENSATIONAL GAME IN BARNSLEY'S HISTORY

Barnsley 2–3 Liverpool
28 March 1998

Not necessarily a violent game but, astonishingly, Barnsley ended up with eight men taking on Liverpool. Referee Gary Willard also decided to leave the field at one stage, taking his assistants with him for a five-minute spell. The referee, fearing for his and the other officials' safety, decided to scarper, leaving a confused group of players wondering what the hell was going on. But what had led to such a sensational state of affairs?

The first half had been a hard-fought encounter, with Barnsley desperate for points to help them escape the relegation zone and Liverpool still hopeful of securing a place in Europe the following season. When the teams ran out for the second half, the game was finely balanced at 1-1. The game erupted in the fifty-third minute when Darren Barnard, who had been struggling to cope with Michael Owen's pace all afternoon, brought down the Liverpool youngster as he homed in on goal. The referee had no hesitation in showing Barnard the red card. Chris Morgan of Barnsley was next to go for appearing to elbow Michael Owen. By this stage the Barnsley supporters were going berserk, and one burly Yorkshireman ran on the pitch and headed for the referee. It was at this stage that the referee and his assistants decided to head for the safety of the dressing-room. Another Barnsley fan decided to vent his anger by running on to the pitch, only for both invaders to be stopped in their tracks by rugby tackles from Fjortoft of Barnsley and Ince of Liverpool.

Eventually, order was restored and the match restarted. The home fans had picked out Michael Owen to vent their venom at and a chant of 'Cheat, cheat' was directed at him for the remainder of the game.

Barnsley had yet another player sent off near the end when Sheridan clashed with Paul Ince after McManaman had scored to give Liverpool a 3-2 lead. Barnsley, who hadn't had a player sent off all season, now had three red-carded in one game for the first time in their history. It is doubtful that Oakwell will witness such a game ever again.

MICHAEL OWEN SEES
HIS BACKSIDE

Manchester United 1-1 Liverpool
2 April 1998

This Good Friday showdown between reigning champions Manchester United and their bitter rivals Liverpool was as hard-fought and downright nasty as most of these games have tended to be over the years. United were looking good to retain their title and Liverpool were desperate to remain in contention.

Michael Owen had just been voted the PFA Young Player of the Year for the 1997/98 season. A few months later the kid from

Hawarden would be the talk of football after his World Cup exploits, but for the time being he was busy making a name for himself as British football's hottest new talent. Pitting his skills against the likes of Manchester United was right up his street and he was determined to make his mark.

United knew that Owen was dangerous and they set out to put him off his game right from the start. Peter Schmeichel headed the queue of United defenders bad-mouthing the Liverpool teenager. Owen initially ignored their remarks and he hit them where it really hurt with a stunning thirtieth-minute equaliser after Ronny Johnson had put United ahead in the eleventh minute. Schmeichel's crude jibes did make some impression on Owen though, and he was cautioned by the referee for a nasty challenge on the Manchester United goalkeeper.

After his well-taken equaliser, Michael Owen and his Liverpool teammates were on a high. They knew they had to beat United to stay in the title race and at this stage of the game were looking the better team. Owen's elation at putting his team back in the game turned to despair just minutes later when he hit Johnson with a brutal challenge. The United defender was left in a heap on the Old Trafford turf and Michael Owen was shown the red card. This was Owen's second dismissal during the 1997/98 season, having previously been sent off for aiming a headbutt at a Yugoslavia defender when playing for England Under-18s in September 1997.

Liverpool's ten men hung on for a valiant point, but all the headlines were centred on Michael Owen's red card. Liverpool boss Roy Evans told the press that Owen had been the subject of some dreadful jibes during the game, but that it was all part and parcel of being a professional footballer. Evans said, 'The sending off was nobody's fault but his own. He got wound up, made two impetuous challenges through sheer enthusiasm and the ref was correct to send him off.' United boss, Alex Ferguson, remarked, 'It was a terrible tackle. Michael Owen is a terrific player, but he doesn't need to do that.' Michael Owen himself had no doubts that he deserved to be sent off and he apologised to Ronny Johnson after the game. Watching

England manager Glenn Hoddle said that the youngster would learn from his mistakes. He said, 'It was a mistimed tackle, the type that happens all around the country every weekend. There was nothing callous about it.'

WHEN PUSH COMES TO SHOVE

Sheffield Wednesday 1-0 Arsenal
26 September 1998

Paulo Di Canio was no stranger to controversy. The Italian could either be sensational because of the quality of his football, or cause a sensation for some crazy misdemeanour on the field of play. This September 1998 fixture was to see Di Canio hit the headlines for the latter. Sheffield Wednesday paid £4.5 million for Di Canio in 1997 and the Italian was proving to be a fine capture, scoring 12 goals during the 1997/98 season. Playing against Arsenal during this period was always going to be a tough, physical encounter and the Gunners had already had two players sent off during the early weeks of the new season.

The game itself was not a memorable encounter from a football point of view. Lee Briscoe won the points for Wednesday with a goal in the last minute, but before that we had a football rarity, a referee being pushed to the ground. Di Canio became involved in a flare-up that began with Patrick Vieira shoving Wednesday's Wim Jonk. Di Canio was alleged to have kicked Martin Keown in the fracas. The Arsenal defender then pushed Di Canio away with his elbow. The referee, Paul Alcock, immediately showed Di Canio and Keown the red card for their part in the rumpus. Di Canio then appeared to push the referee, who lost his balance and tumbled to the ground. It was hardly an all-out attack on the official by the Italian, but the mere fact that he dared to shove a referee was something of a sensation at the time.

When the game ended there was another incident when Patrick Vieira was alleged to have made a rude gesture to the crowd and then become involved in a tussle with a policeman in the tunnel after the match. Apparently Vieira felt a hand on his shoulder and, not realising it was a police officer, swung out an arm to ward off what he thought was a possible attacker.

The aftermath of Di Canio's push on the referee was headline news for days. Brendon Batson, the deputy chief executive of the Professional Footballers' Association, said, 'No matter what case Di Canio puts forward, the evidence is damning. I think the book will be thrown at him with some force.' Philip Don, the Premiership referees' spokesman, told reporters, 'I hope the FA will take strong action on Di Canio. Paul Alcock is very shocked. It is something you don't expect to happen. When things like this happen you have to consider your place in the game. I hope that Paul will be able to carry on as a top referee.'

The volatile Di Canio received a lengthy ban from the English game for his moment of madness.

THREE HAMMERS SENT OFF

West Ham United 1–5 Leeds United
1 May 1999

West Ham had three players sent off in this violent end-of-season encounter. What with the training-ground bust-up between Hartson and Berkovic, when cameras caught Hartson kicking his teammate in the face, and other misdemeanours, the season had not been a great one for the Hammers on the disciplinary front. Leeds were desperate for the points to secure a place in next season's UEFA Cup and, despite the mayhem going on all around them, managed to keep their mind on the job in hand.

Ian Wright was booked in the opening stages of the game for elbowing Alf-Inge Haaland. Then, after fifteen minutes, he was sent off following an off-the-ball incident with Ian Harte. The referee's assistant, who had pointed out Wright's misdemeanour to the referee, was then confronted by several threatening West Ham fans, but stewards moved in quickly to protect him. Referee Rob Harris then red-carded West Ham goalkeeper Shaka Hislop for bringing down Jimmy Floyd Hasselbaink. Harte scored from the spot to give Leeds a 3-1 lead. It was now nine men against eleven and West Ham tempers were still rising.

Leeds, using their numerical advantage to good effect, scored two more goals before a third West Ham player was sent off. Steve Lomas was the man, dismissed for a crude lunge at Ian Harte. For the first time in their history, West Ham had had three players sent off in a game.

The trouble didn't end there. After the game it was alleged that Ian Wright had kicked in the door to the referee's dressing-room and vandalised the area. Another day out at an FA disciplinary hearing was on the cards for the volatile striker. West Ham manager Harry Redknapp was dumbfounded. 'That referee lost the plot completely,' was all Harry would say.

CLASH OF THE TITANS: VIEIRA *v.* KEANE

Arsenal 1-2 Manchester United
21 August 1999

Patrick Vieira's decision to join Juventus at the start of the 2005/06 season robbed the Premiership of one of its great spectacles; Roy Keane taking on Patrick Vieira in a battle for midfield supremacy was a sight to behold. Back in August 1999 the two best teams in the country produced a breathtaking game of football before a violent set-to at the finish threatened to escalate into an all-out brawl. With

United's Roy Keane and Arsenal's Patrick Vieira locking horns in a battle royal of the top two midfield enforcers in British football, an explosion was likely to occur at any time. During a pulsating first half the crowd held its breath when Keane hacked Vieira down as he strode away from him. The referee took no action, preferring to keep the momentum of the game flowing

With Arsenal leading 1–0 at the break through a Freddie Ljungberg goal, there was no let-up in the action in the second half as both teams pressed for goals. Keane equalised for United as the action grew more electric and physical by the minute. The anticipated clash between Vieira and Keane did occur in a midfield tussle for the ball, but on this occasion the Irishman decided to back off. Manchester United then took the lead through Keane's second goal and this galvanised Arsenal into searching for an equaliser.

By the final stages of the game the action had become decidedly more physical, and United goalkeeper Raimond van der Gouw had to be stretchered off after Martin Keown had clattered into him attempting to get the ball over the line. A melee then erupted in the United penalty area and Vieira was seen to butt Keane before pushing him in the face with the palm of his hand. Keane then grabbed Vieira by the throat and Jaap Stam also joined in the rumpus, but still no action was taken by the referee. The whistle for time was blown and in the 'hardest footballer in the Premier League' showdown between Keane and Vieira, the Frenchman probably took the title on points. Manchester United, however, took the three points that really mattered.

Liverpool's Steven Gerrard, now established as one of the best midfielders in the world, let alone the Premiership, but at the time still in the shadow of Keane and Vieira, said:

> It's always explosive when United play Arsenal. Keane and Vieira haven't just been the top midfielders in England, they have probably been the best two in the world. Being a Liverpool fan and Scouser, I'm not supposed to admit this, but Roy Keane has been my favourite player over the past ten years or so.

A LITTLE SPAT AT ANFIELD

Liverpool 0–1 Everton
27 September 1999

Merseyside derby games are generally white-hot affairs, but this was something else. Three players were red-carded as the game exploded into a frenzy of fist fights, career-threatening tackles and general mayhem. As usual, both teams were totally committed from the start and the football was fast, furious and passionate.

Three Liverpool players found themselves in referee Mike Riley's notebook during the opening half: Owen, Redknapp and Staunton, all for reckless tackles. Owen, in fact, was lucky not to receive a red card after he aimed an ugly two-footed lunge at David Weir that could have inflicted serious damage on the Everton defender. Everton's Don Hutchison should also have walked during the first half for an x-rated tackle on Dietmar Hamann that did not even receive a booking.

If the first half was bad, the second was even worse. There had been a brief bust-up between Liverpool goalkeeper Sander Westerveld and Everton's Francis Jeffers in the first half, but they decided to go for the real thing in the seventy-fifth minute and a flurry of punches were exchanged between the two. 'Francis must have thrown twenty punches and not one of them landed,' joked Everton boss Walter Smith after the game. But both players had to go. It was alleged after the game that Jeffers released a volley of spit at the Liverpool keeper and this contributed to Westerveld blowing his top.

With Everton clinging on to a one-goal lead, the bone-crunching tackles continued to fly in unabated and Liverpool's up-and-coming youngster Steven Gerrard was dismissed after going in studs-first on Everton's goalscorer Kevin Campbell. Everton held on to record a hard-fought victory.

Liverpool boss Gerard Houllier was furious with his team's lack of self-discipline, saying to the press, 'How can you control the game if you don't control yourself. Never mind that you have been provoked and you've been hit. You have to keep cool. Some of my team lost the plot.'

KICKING AND SPITTING AT UPTON PARK

West Ham United 2-1 Arsenal
3 October 1999

At the end of this pulsating London derby the crime count was two sent off and eight other players booked. Red cards went to Vieira of Arsenal and Foé of West Ham. Yellow cards were dished out to Bergkamp, Keown, Henry and Grimandi of Arsenal, and West Ham's Lomas, Wanchope, Stimac and Moncur. Apart from the passion of the tackling and the sheer drama of the football on offer, the game will mainly be remembered for the Vieira spitting incident.

Football in England is a game in which you can break someone's leg (deliberately in some cases), elbow someone's teeth out, and dish out all manner of physical violence, and though there might be a brief period of uproar by football fans and pundits, you will soon be forgiven. Commit the cardinal sin of spitting at an opponent and you are scum. The lowest of the low.

The supremely gifted but highly volatile Vieira had already received a booking earlier in the game. After an eightieth-minute foul on West Ham's Di Canio, the French international lost all semblance of self-control when the red card was shown to him. It looked at one stage as if he was going to take a swing at the referee, before first Neil Ruddock and then Frank Lampard became the focal point for his grievance. Wind-up merchant Ruddock received a mouthful of spit in his face for his troubles.

As Vieira was escorted down the tunnel it was alleged that he even had a poke at a policeman. 'I was only trying to calm things down,' claimed that well-known peacemaker Neil Ruddock. 'What he did was scum, the worst of all things. The coppers should have knocked his f—ing head off.' West Ham's Marc Vivien Foé then took Dennis Bergkamp out with a brutal challenge and he too received a red card for a second bookable offence.

West Ham held on to win a sensational London derby 2-1. But the game will be remembered mainly for the flare-up after the spitting incident, for which Vieira apologised after the game. He told reporters, 'Nothing can excuse what I did. Spitting at an opponent is a terrible thing to do. I have had it done to me and it's dreadful. I have never done anything like that before.' Asked why he did it, he said, 'Ruddock provoked me. He pushed me over and called me a French prat.' West Ham manager Harry Redknapp remarked, 'Vieira knows what he did was out of order. But I've met him off the park and he's a smashing lad. He just lost it on Sunday.'

For his moment of madness, Vieira was fined £45,000 and banned for six games by the FA. Arsène Wenger was unhappy at the FA's decision and told the press, 'The punishment is very severe, Patrick is not a dirty player. His attitude is right and I don't think that this will affect his aggression on the field.'

USING YOUR HEAD AT UPTON PARK

West Ham United 1-1 Sunderland
24 October 1999

Yet another stormy game at West Ham, with the team who were taking the Premiership by storm, Sunderland, looking for their sixth straight win on the trot. From the kick-off this was a bad-tempered encounter and after twenty minutes the bust-up that had threatened from the start occurred when West Ham's Costa Rican forward Paulo Wanchope fell to the ground clutching his head. Referee Mark Halsey failed to spot what had caused Wanchope's injury, but one of his assistants had seen the incident. Veteran Sunderland defender Steve Bould was called to the referee and shown the red card. It emerged that Bould was dismissed for appearing to headbutt Wanchope.

In the skirmishing that followed Bould's sending-off, Wanchope got to his feet and became involved in a tussle with Sunderland's Paul Butler. Butler alleged that Wanchope spat in his face, but eventually the two sets of players calmed down and the game restarted.

There was then an incident involving West Ham's Trevor Sinclair and Sunderland's Alex Rae. Sinclair claimed that his lip was cut when Rae elbowed him in the face. The Sunderland player said the collision with Sinclair was accidental. Whatever the cause was, Sinclair left the field for treatment and was only persuaded to return after treatment. 'If I hadn't gone off to cool down I would probably ripped someone's head off,' said Sinclair after the game. Ten-man Sunderland held on for a 1-1 draw.

West Ham's manager Harry Redknapp, speaking about the game's controversial incidents said, 'I'm told that Steve Bould used his head on Paulo. His eye came up like a balloon.' As for spitting claims, Redknapp remarked, 'I didn't see anything. If Wanchope did spit at anyone I'd hit him with a heavy fine.' Sunderland boss Peter Reid said, 'I'm a manager who likes to keep everything in-house. Steve Bould made an error of judgement and I'll be fining him.'

CRETINOUS BEHAVIOUR
AT THE BRIDGE

Chelsea 2-1 Leicester City
FA Cup
30 January 2000

Bad blood between these two teams goes back a few seasons and this FA Cup encounter was the day it finally spilled over into violence on the pitch and bad-mouthing each other off it. The first half was a typical no-holds-barred cup tie, with the first flashpoint coming when Dennis Wise, never a player to be put off by the prospect of taking on someone twice his size, decided to make his mark on Leicester's resident hard man Steve Walsh by stamping on the veteran defender and raking his studs down his shin for good measure. For this horror tackle, Wise was booked. One thing was certain: Walsh would gain painful retribution on a Chelsea player before the game was over. The strange thing is it was not to be inflicted on the player who had wronged him in the first place, Dennis Wise.

Chelsea, who took a one-goal advantage into the second half, increased their lead with a disputed Weah strike. Leicester claimed that Chris Sutton fouled Phil Gilchrist before passing for Weah to score, but the goal stood. Leicester defender Steve Walsh was now thrown up front in an attempt to snatch a goal back. The game finally came to a boil when Walsh felt someone tugging at his shirt and lashed out with his elbow. Unfortunately for Walsh, his flailing elbow connected with Chris Sutton's chin and the referee sent the Leicester player off for the eleventh time in his career.

Dennis Wise then received the red card that his first half horror tackle on Walsh had deserved, after a second yellow card for a handball offence. Chelsea held on to win 2-1 to progress into the FA Cup quarter-finals. Relations between the two clubs, however, were at an all-time low.

Recriminations carried on after the game with Leicester manager Martin O'Neill branding Chelsea's mouthy chairman Ken Bates a 'footballing cretin' for comments that Bates made about the Leicester team. O'Neill was so infuriated that he even stopped his midfield player Robbie Savage from swapping shirts with Chelsea's French star Marcel Desailly after the game, bringing back memories of similar actions by Alf Ramsey after a violent encounter with Argentina during the 1966 World Cup.

Defending his team against accusations that his Leicester team were at times over-physical, O'Neill claimed that Chelsea were also capable of dishing it out and said, 'It's a fallacy to think that Chelsea are not prepared to mix it. They know how to look after themselves.'

Asked if Sutton had recovered from his collision with Walsh's elbow, Chelsea boss Gianluca Vialli smiled and said, 'He will be ready to fight Mike Tyson next month.'

THE BRIDGE OF SIGHS

Chelsea 3–1 Wimbledon
12 February 2000

Saturday 12 February 2000 was a day of passion and fury in the Premiership. There was a mass brawl at Elland Road when a brutal Lee Bowyer tackle on Spurs' Stephen Clemence caused a twenty-man ruck that threatened to boil out of control. When the dust settled, Bowyer was lucky to get away with just a caution and a stern lecture from the referee. At St James' Park Roy Keane was sent off for a late tackle on Robert Lee and Andy Cole and Jaap Stam were booked during Manchester United's defeat by Newcastle.

The real nasty stuff however, took place at Stamford Bridge. Chelsea's encounters against Wimbledon have produced some tasty affairs over the years and this was no exception. From the start Chelsea's Dennis Wise and Wimbledon's Kenny Cunningham had been involved in little niggles. In the main the referee managed to prevent this particular vendetta bursting out of control. The game itself was a hard-fought affair with the Wimbledon defence keeping the Chelsea attack at bay until ten minutes from the end. It was Wimbledon, in fact, who had snatched the lead on seventy-two minutes when Lund scored from a Cort pass. This sparked Chelsea into action and three late goals gave them a comfortable victory in the end.

Before the final whistle blew, Wise and Cunningham were once again at each other's throats and the argument carried on as the two teams left the field of play and entered the tunnel. What happened next is unclear. Some accounts suggested that in the general melee that ensued, punches were thrown and apart from Wise and Cunningham, there were other participants.

Chelsea manager Gianluca Vialli and Wimbledon coach Mick Harford were seen to be involved in a furious argument. Egil Olsen, the Wimbledon manager, found himself being pinned up against a wall before he managed to escape the madness going on all around him. At this stage, referee Peter Jones was running around furiously blowing his whistle in an attempt to restore order. When eventually the two opposing teams made their way to their respective dressing-rooms, few were prepared to discuss what had actually taken place. The Chelsea assistant manager Gwyn Jones told the press, 'Someone fell down the steps. There was nothing in it, just a little scuffle.'

Vialli, however, was a little more revealing. He said, 'I can tell you that something happened, but we don't want to say anything official at the moment. We will wait for the referee to decide what he wants to put in his report. Definitely something did happen, but I think it is better to keep it quiet.' Dennis Wise was also reluctant to talk about the incident. 'Why do you lot always want to talk to me about fights?' he blurted, before returning to the Chelsea dressing-room.

The following day the Wimbledon captain Robbie Earle revealed that a bust-up did take place in the tunnel. He said, 'There was a difference of opinion in the tunnel, more push and shove than anything. There was a lot of shouting and the referee was there blowing his whistle before we got separated. Let's just say that there was a little more action than the last Mike Tyson fight.'

THE BATTLE OF THE BUFFET

Manchester United 2–0 Arsenal
24 October 2004

'The only trouble we have, regarding violence in modern-day football, is that there just isn't enough.' These sentiments were recently expressed by a top Premiership player. It's true that violent encounters are not quite as frequent as days gone by. Amongst the exceptions to the rule, however, have been the totally engrossing games during the past few seasons between Manchester United and Arsenal.

Sadly for fans of x-rated football, the 2005 FA Cup final between the two clubs was somewhat of a damp squib. Arsenal won the trophy, rather fortunately, but the eagerly anticipated no-holds-barred bloodbath between the two warring factions failed to materialise. The game obviously came under close scrutiny by the FA. With the game televised live throughout the world, the two teams were warned not to let the showpiece occasion degenerate into another brawl.

The concern of the FA had been aroused by the two meetings between Manchester United and Arsenal in the Premiership during the 2004/05 season. The October 2004 game has now gone down in football folklore as 'The Battle of the Buffet' due to the incredible goings-on in the tunnel at Old Trafford after the game.

Arsenal were bidding to extend their unbeaten run in the Premiership to 50 games. United were desperate for the points in order to keep in touch with Arsenal at the top of the table. As usual in United–Arsenal matches, the tackles were flying in right from the start. Ruud van Nistelrooy was lucky not to be sent off after raking the studs of his boot down Ashley Cole's leg. Arsenal's Jose Antonio Reyes was also on the receiving end of some crude United tackles and Rio Ferdinand could have received his marching orders for a professional foul on Freddie Ljungberg.

Manchester United were fortunate to find referee Mike Riley in a lenient mood and Arsenal's boss Arsène Wenger was further enraged when Wayne Rooney won a dubious penalty kick. With United already leading 1-0, Rooney appeared to dive when Sol Campbell poked his leg near him but failed to make contact. Van Nistelrooy wrapped up the game for United from the spot-kick.

When the final whistle blew, a furious Arsène Wenger, feeling his team had been cheated, became involved in a bitter tunnel bust-up. Arsenal's Thierry Henry had already become embroiled in a slanging match on the pitch with United goalkeeper Roy Carroll, which resulted in Henry pursuing Carroll into the tunnel in order to continue their disagreement. Sir Alex Ferguson was then hit by food thrown by the Arsenal players. An eyewitness said that Ferguson was covered in soup and pizza and had to change his shirt for a television interview. There were even claims that Wenger challenged Ferguson to a stand-up fight in the tunnel.

When the dust had settled after Old Trafford's Battle of the Buffet, Arsène Wenger was fined £15,000 by the FA for his accusation that Ruud van Nistelrooy was a cheat. Van Nistelrooy also received a three-match ban for his crude tackle on Ashley Cole.

Sir Alex Ferguson was still bitter about the whole affair months later and he told the press:

> In the tunnel Wenger was publicly calling my players cheats. I went out into the tunnel and told him to behave himself. He came sprinting towards me with his hands raised saying, 'What do you want to do about it?' To not apologise for the behaviour

Arsenal manager Arsène Wenger advises Manchester United boss Sir Alex Ferguson to watch out for flying pizza after their teams' October 2004 encounter.

of his players to another manager is a disgrace, but I don't expect Wenger ever to apologise.

THE TUNNEL OF HATE

Arsenal 2–4 Manchester United
1 February 2005

Chelsea deservedly won the League title for the second time in their history in 2005, but the game of the season did not involve them. It took place at Highbury on a cold Tuesday evening at the beginning of February. This game was simply sensational. It had everything: great tackles, great goals and, above all, passion. But the real drama started before the game had even kicked off. Millions of television viewers could not believe their eyes when they witnessed the sight of Roy Keane challenging Arsenal's hardman Patrick Vieira to a fight on the pitch before the evenings proceedings had begun.

Apparently Keane overheard Vieira dishing out threats to United's Gary Neville while the two sets of players lined up in the tunnel. Roy Keane told Vieira to lay off Neville and that he would meet him on the pitch if he wanted to sort it out. Thinking better of it, Vieira then decided to take refuge behind referee Graham Poll just in case Keane decided to take the matter further. The sight of 6ft 4in Vieira backing off from 5ft 10in Keane certainly gave the watching millions pause for thought as they waited for the imminent battle of English football's premier hardmen to take place on the pitch. When the game began, the expected flare-up between Keane and Vieira failed to materialise, but if it had it seemed that there would only ever be one winner – and it wouldn't be the Arsenal midfielder.

The game itself was a classic, with Manchester United ending any hopes that Arsenal may have had of catching Chelsea at the top of the Premiership. In between the great football, clashes did take place, between Bergkamp and Carroll and Rooney and Lauren. Mikael Silvestre, for no apparent reason, headbutted Freddie Ljungberg and was sent off with twenty minutes of the game remaining. Ljungberg was left with a bloody nose.

Asked about the incident in the tunnel before the game started, Roy Keane told reporters, 'Patrick Vieira is 6ft 4in and was having a go at Gary Neville, so I said, "Have a go at me." If Vieira wants to intimidate our players and thinks that Gary Neville is an easy target, I'm not having it.'

Vieira told the press that he didn't threaten anyone. He said, 'They are big enough players to handle themselves. Gary Neville is a big lad – he can handle himself. I had a talk with Roy Keane and that's it.' But football fans throughout the land were left in little doubt that the boy from Cork definitely won this particular battle of English football's top midfield enforcers.

Later that year, before a World Cup qualifier between the Republic of Ireland and France, Vieira said:

I know Roy Keane well. There has always been tension between us on the pitch, but we respect each other. I know he will be tough with me and I will be tough with him too. He is a very determined man, like me. It always ended with us shaking hands at the end of the match.

THE THRILLA AGAINST THE VILLA: LEE BOWYER v. KIERON DYER

Newcastle United 0–3 Aston Villa
2 April 2005

This end-of-season encounter between two of the Premiership's underachievers began the afternoon as one of the most inconsequential fixtures of the day. Newcastle had managed to string together a 13-game unbeaten run but, like Villa, they looked destined to end the season as Premiership also-rans. Newcastle were expected to take the points, but Aston Villa had other plans and Juan Pablo Angel put them into an early lead. Newcastle laid siege to the Villa goal, but squandered a series of good goalscoring opportunities.

The second half sprung into life when referee Barry Knight sent off Newcastle's Steven Taylor for handling a goal-bound Villa effort in the penalty area. Gareth Barry slotted home the spot-kick and scored Aston Villa's third just eight minutes later, also from a penalty kick.

The surprise scoreline on Tyneside was of slight interest to the rest of the country, but what happened in the eighty-second minute at St James' Park has gone down in football history as one of the most bizarre bust-ups in the game's history. Lee Bowyer and Kieron Dyer, who had been two of United's better performers in a poor Newcastle display, became embroiled in a sensational punch-up in the middle of the pitch. The flare-up started when Dyer ignored Bowyer and passed the ball to another Newcastle team-mate. Bowyer launched himself at Dyer with a flurry of punches and the startled Newcastle forward initially struggled to defend himself before hitting back with a few blows himself. The feuding pair's astonished teammates quickly intervened and brought the middleweight battle of St James' Park to an abrupt end. The extraordinary Bowyer–Dyer dust-up lasted only a matter of seconds, but it was the talk of football that Saturday evening

Watching Lee Bowyer, Graeme Souness and Kieron Dyer washing Newcastle United's dirty linen in public after the infamous Bowyer–Dyer punch-up in April 2005 made better Saturday evening television entertainment than *The X Factor* for most viewers. Bowyer ended up being fined £250,000 by Newcastle for his part in the brawl.

and was headline news for days to come. The referee had no other option than to send Bowyer and Dyer off, making Newcastle the first Premiership team to have three players sent off since West Ham had three dismissed in their May 1999 clash against Leeds.

After the game the Newcastle manager, Graeme Souness, made Bowyer and Dyer appear at a press conference to apologise for their behaviour. Souness sat by the shame-faced pair as they issued their heart-wrenching apologies to the Newcastle fans for letting them down. Souness was as surprised as the incredulous football public by the flare-up and remarked, 'There's no problem between Lee and Kieron. There has been the odd argument in training, but that's as far as it goes.'

However, Newcastle's captain and living legend Alan Shearer was livid, Putting his own dust-ups of the past to the back of his memory he launched a scathing attack on Bowyer and Dyer. He said, 'Our dirty linen has been hung out for the country to witness yet again. What happened was a disgrace. There is no defence for it and I made my feelings known in the dressing-room. The good name of Newcastle is being dragged through the dirt.'

Alan Shearer may well have been appalled by the behaviour of Bowyer and Dyer but outside of Newcastle, football fans from far and wide found the punch-up great entertainment. It is also highly likely that if a rematch could be arranged for some time in the near future, television rights would soon be snapped up by broadcasting companies.

AN ABUNDANCE OF HANDBAGS AT DAWN

Rangers 3–1 Celtic
20 August 2005

The 2005/06 season was just a few weeks old when the Old Firm clash between Rangers and Celtic came up trumps again in terms of bad blood in derby matches. Merseyside, London, Manchester, the Midlands and the North-East have all had their fair share of unsavoury local encounters but they are, and never have been, a match for Glasgow's finest.

Celtic finished the game with two red cards and two yellow. Rangers could only manage three yellow cards, but with most of the season still to go, there was still plenty of time for the Ibrox boys to catch them up. Reigning champions Rangers, with Alex McLeish at the helm, were already odds-on favourites to take a second successive title with only a couple of games played. Celtic boss Gordon Strachan, new to the manager's role at Celtic Park, looked to be in danger of getting the push after just a few games.

There was a lot riding on this game for Strachan's team after their early exit from the Champions' League in the qualifying rounds. The early stages of the game were relatively uneventful, but all hell broke loose in the twenty-third minute when Thompson brought down Nacho Novo with a tackle from behind. The Celtic forward was dispatched to the dressing-room by referee Stuart Dougal. Ten minutes later Rangers took the lead when Dado Prso latched on to a pass from Andrews and volleyed the ball home.

Rangers increased their lead early in the second half when Buffel knocked in goal number two. With Celtic staring defeat in the face in the first Old Firm clash of the season, Strachan's team's tempers began to fray. Neil Lennon said after the game that he had come in for an incredible amount of stick from both the Rangers players and also the Ibrox crowd throughout the whole game. The Celtic midfielder was booked by the referee in the seventieth minute for a display of petulance, but this was only the forerunner of worse things to come. Maloney gave Celtic hope with an eighty-sixth-minute penalty, but Novo wrapped up the three points for Rangers with a spot-kick two minutes later.

Neil Lennon had threatened to explode during the second period and when the referee blew for time he made his way to the officials. Lennon's Celtic teammates had to hold him back as he attempted to tell Stuart Dougal and his two assistants that he wouldn't be sending them Christmas cards this year. Lennon was then red-carded for abusing the referee as teammate Paul Telfer held onto him in an attempt to stop the Celtic star finding himself in even worse trouble. Gordon Strachan told the press later, 'Neil Lennon never swore at the ref directly. It was only industrial language. He told the ref he wasn't very enamoured with the performance.'

In the aftermath of the game Rangers' Nacho Novo refused to condemn Alan Thompson for his tackle on him. He said, 'I don't know if Thompson's challenge was a red card offence. You always get really hard tackles in Old Firm games. Our manager told us what an emotional occasion the game against Celtic could be and he warned us to keep our discipline.'

The Scottish Football Association, however, had no doubts that Thompson's red card was warranted. Donald McVicar, head of referee development at the SFA, said, 'The referee did the job the SFA want him to do. Thompson's tackle on Nove comes into the career-threatening category.' As for Lennon's outburst at the end of the game, both the Celtic chief executive and Lennon himself issued statements of apology. Celtic's Peter Lawwell said, 'Neil has apologised and we know his reaction was wrong. He has been an excellent servant to this club over the past five years and he deserves the appropriate level of support.'

Neil Lennon told the press, 'Clearly, although I felt the red card was unjustified, I understand my reaction was wrong. I apologise for my reaction towards the referee and his assistant and I also apologise to Celtic and our supporters.' Lennon received a six-match ban for his misdemeanour.

BIBLIOGRAPHY

Sunday Telegraph
Daily Telegraph
Sunday Mirror
The Mirror
The Times
The Guardian
Sunday People
Daily Express
The Sunday Post
The Liverpool Daily Post
The Liverpool Echo
Four Four Two
Rothmans Football Yearbook 1970-2000
The Sunday Times Illustrated History of Football 1995
Golden Heroes: Fifty Seasons of Footballer of the Year, Dennis Signy and
    Norman Giller, Chameleon Books 1997
My Autobiography, Kevin Keegan, Warner Books 1997
Life at the Kop, Phil Neal, Queen Anne Press 1986
Behind the Network: My Autobiography, Bob Wilson, Coronet Books
    2003
Blowing the Whistle, Toni Schumacher, W.H. Allen & Co. 1990
Shades of Gray, Andy Gray, Queen Anne Press 1986

Wembley: The Greatest Stage, Tom Watt and Kevin Palmer, Simon & Schuster 1998

Do That Again Son and I'll Break Your Legs, Phil Thompson, Virgin 1996

England: The Alf Ramsey Years, Graham McColl, Chameleon Books 1998

A Celtic A-Z, Tom Campbell and Pat Woods, Greenfield Press 1992

Special thanks to James Howarth, Holly Bennion
and all at Tempus Publishing